DAYS WE HAVE SEEN

An Englishman's personal account of his family's experiences in war-torn Cyprus during 1974 and 1975

Peter Moore

Copyright © 2013 Peter Moore

All rights reserved.

ISBN: -10: 1482687658
ISBN: -13: 978-1482687651

Cover design by Paul-Faizi Moore

Photographs processed by Vassos Stylianou

For my sons, Zim and Tom

CONTENTS

	Foreword	v
	Map of Cyprus in 2013	ix
	Acknowledgements	x
	Preface	Page 11
Chapter 1	War and Evacuation	Page 15
Chapter 2	England	Page 29
Chapter 3	Return to Cyprus	Page 33
Chapter 4	The School	Page 39
Chapter 5	Kolossi Camp	Page 49
Chapter 6	Leaving the Camp	Page 121
	Postscript	Page 125

Foreword

I met Peter Moore just over 40 years ago, back in 1972. He had just moved from the UK to Famagusta, my hometown, with his wife May and their two-year-old son Paul-Faizi. Ready for a new life. Ready for a new experience. Why Famagusta? Was it the sea, was it the small and quiet town, was it the magic of a Mediterranean resort, or was it the life tempo or the people he hardly knew…

Peter was a young teacher in his late twenties at the time and I was soon to finish the high school. My decision to study photography in the UK was long made before I met the young teacher. In order to be accepted in a photography course, a selection of GCE certificates including English language was a must. But the subject that would really make the difference and open the doors to the top universities and colleges of art and technology was a GCE certificate in Art. So, Peter had now one of his first students and I had my first art teacher.

From the first lesson and during the two years that followed until August 1974, in Famagusta, Peter and his family were to become very dear friends. We established a relationship far beyond that of a teacher - student. My eyes were opened into new forms of art. I saw for the first time some nail sculptures that Peter prepared and arranged methodically and accurately. Thirty years later, as a professional, I photographed some of the nail sculptures of the late Christoforos Savva, the pioneer in Cyprus Contemporary Art. These photographs were used in a high quality publication with some of the artist's best work. It's only then that I realised that the similar works of the two artists were made just 4-5 years apart.

The house of Peter and May was always open for me. My friends were also welcome. People were not afraid of burglars at the time. The small window of the front door was left half open all day long. All you had to do was just to push your hand through and open the door from the inside. No locked doors. Cyprus hospitality and way of life, at its best. At least once a week, usually on Friday nights there was an open house at Peter's. All the guests would bring a dish for an international cuisine night. I remember those beautiful summer evenings full of music and such relaxation. Endless discussions on so many topics... art, life, philosophy and in the background a darts and a table tennis competition in progress.

In August 1974 the happy life of the people of Famagusta came to a sudden end. The suitcases of Peter and his family were not full of dreams and excitement for the unknown, now. This time, their small suitcases were packed with very few basic supplies for emergency survival. Peter and his family fled Famagusta in exactly the same way the rest of the Cypriots did. Two years proved ample time for Peter and his family to become and to feel "Cypriots". They refused to be treated in a special way, even though it was very easy for them since they were British. They lived the evacuation minute by minute and shared the agony, the pain and devastation of their fellow citizens. They drove out of Famagusta towards the south with the minimum of their belongings like we all did, thinking that they would return to their homes after a few days when it would be safe again.

Soon after, Peter found himself and his family safe in England. Within three months they made their way back to Cyprus. He felt that they were also refugees and that he was obliged to return to the island to find out about the fate of their friends and to help them in any possible way they could. To use his own words: "Cyprus was calling us in a way I have found difficult to explain to bewildered family and friends. There was something about the island that made us feel we belonged there."

In this unique book, Peter shares his experiences with his fellow refugees during the troubled years of 1974 and 1975. He describes in extreme detail the life in a school in Limassol, which housed many refugee families and the life at Kolossi Camp, which was to be his family's home for many months.

He was accepted by the refugees as one of them and managed to organize them into groups and to keep them occupied at the same time. His groups managed to produce more than 33,000 replica icons, under his directions and supervision. These icons were to be sold and yield the first income for the people of the camp. At the same time, Peter's wife, May, set up English and handicraft classes for the children. The committee that managed the refugee handicrafts projects eventually became the Cyprus Handicraft Service.

Peter cared for these ordinary people so much. He lived with them during those first, very hard months. They, in return shared with him their distress, their hardship, their daily problems, their fears, their past and their hopes for the future. Peter was always there, a good friend and a good listener, trying to make their life more comfortable. As a social worker, a sports teacher, an event organiser, a food provider, as a fellow citizen. At the same time he carefully observed everything in the camp. The details in his descriptions in this book are exceptional. His stories are so moving and so frank! Stories written for the first time from the heart, stories that marked Peter's life.

The meaning of life unfolds from the pages of Peter's book. The reader will be guided to rediscover the values of the simple daily luxuries of life, through Peter's descriptions of his experiences with the refugees. This book is not another war and politics account. It's about life philosophy, emotions, tranquillity, dignity, a feeling of belonging to a community; it's about solidarity between ordinary people.

The language barrier was present but it proved too weak to stop Peter's will to help his fellow "citizens". During his stay at the camp, Peter took hundreds of photographs recording the life of his fellow refugees. Peter kept these valuable black and white negatives and a selection of these was carefully scanned and processed, to be used in the book. The detail that was revealed from the negatives was amazing.

When Peter saw the first final scans on my monitor, he was shocked and burst into tears. These people came alive in front of his eyes after all these years and he was reliving the 1974 - 1975 camp life one more time.

Peter experimented in many forms of art using a vast range of materials, from wood sculptures to nail sculptures, from wax to glass and metal. His life passion was ceramics. He went back to university in 1988 for a postgraduate diploma in ceramics. He became a senior lecturer at a college in the UK and eventually gained an MA for practising artists.

Upon retiring he returned to Cyprus with his wife May, where he lives and works on his new ceramic creations. Our friendship is blessed with very strong bonds from our past based on mutual respect. Even if we don't see each other as much as we would like, nothing can change our feelings.

Was Cyprus the ideal choice for Peter Moore and his family? Did he ever regret his first decision to move from UK to Famagusta in 1972? The answers to these questions, and many more one might have, will be answered in the pages of the book..

Vassos Stylianou
Limassol, Cyprus 2013

This not just another account of the war in Cyprus in 1974. It is exceptional because it is written by an artist who is both a detached outside observer and a passionate insider who cares very much for the well-being of Cypriots, Greek and Turkish alike. Though the author gives a clear objective background account of the politics that brought about the war, his main focus is on how it affected ordinary people. This personal account of the war and its immediate aftermath is brought to life by the author's artistic sensitivity to alternating feelings of fear and calmness and illuminating details of sights, sounds, smells and touch. The story is essentially one of ordinary people, like himself or the reader, living in any country, who are suddenly caught up in the chaos, violence and passions of war. As such it has a universal relevance going far beyond the people of Cyprus. Much of the story is made up of vignettes of mainly humble people rising above adversity and finding happiness and humour in the most difficult circumstances. It is a short book and once picked up it is so compulsive a read that it is impossible to put down until the end is reached.

John Huddleston Florida USA 2013

Cyprus as it is in 2013

ACKNOWLEDGMENTS

It is said that no author ever writes a book alone and that is certainly true of my experience with this book. My grateful thanks for all their help and encouragement go especially to my wife May and my sons Paul-Faizi and Thomas. I would also like to thank Vassos and Maria Stylianou, John Huddleston, Stelios Panayides, Takis Stavri, Paul Moore, Lynne Moore, Naysan and Zohreh Faizi, Shideh Moddaber and Jackie Cowling.

For her unique encouragement and untiring support my heartfelt thanks go to my late mentor, Gloria Faizi .

Preface

We see the pictures all too often in the TV news bulletins; the pilot's view of the ground far below. The electronic systems seek and find the target, crosshairs lock on, the bombs are released and a few seconds later a cloud of dust mushrooms across the screen. We don't see until later, and sometimes not at all, the effects of these remote hi-tech strikes on the people on the ground.

In the same way we can easily forget in the endless play of power politics what happens to ordinary people when political systems fail and countries go to war. What happened in Cyprus in 1974 was, by global superpower standards, a mere miscalculation; but for thousands of Cypriots, both Greek and Turk, it was a disaster.

I want to record the stories of a few of those people, to get down to ground level and show what happens to families like yours and mine when they get caught up in a war. I want to relate what I consider to be the triumph of the human spirit over adversity and the humour that can come through even the most difficult times.

*

In the summer of 1974 everything seemed to be going so well for my family and me. In 1972, at the age of twenty eight, and a newly qualified teacher, I had risked the move from the UK to Cyprus without first securing a teaching post. Cyprus seemed like an ideal choice as we wanted to live in a warmer climate and to be close to my wife's parents who lived at the time in Israel. We also wanted to be close to the sea and settled in Famagusta on the eastern shores of the island. After several months scratching out a hand to mouth existence making decorative candles for the souvenir shops and teaching English privately to small groups of young children, I secured an excellent post as the art teacher at the Famagusta Grammar School.[1]

Despite the rumbling political troubles we had settled comfortably into our new life and were congratulating ourselves on our good fortune when the political situation took a dramatic turn for the worse. A coup d'état was quickly followed by an invasion of the island by mainland Turkish forces and we were forced to leave our home. We became refugees.

My original intention was to write a few short stories about those events in 1974 and 1975. At that time my wife, May, and I, with our four year old son, Paul-Faizi (nicknamed Zim), lived and worked for nearly a year with Greek Cypriot refugees who were, like us, victims of the Turkish invasion. Most of those stories are set in the refugee camp that stood at the eastern edge of the village of Kolossi, near Limassol on the south coast of Cyprus.

Having written the stories, I felt they needed to be put into a context and decided to write about how we came to find ourselves living on a refugee camp and what we did there. As I wrote I realised that the stories would fit well into a roughly chronological account of our experiences and decided to combine context and stories.

Nearly forty years have passed since those events and a mental journey back to them reminds me of the descent from the heights of the Troodos mountains on a cloudy winter's day. At times the way is vague and indistinct but then the clouds suddenly vanish and everything is clear and sharply focussed.

Some details will live with me for the rest of my life and are as clear to me as if they had happened yesterday. Where my memories are clouded and unreliable I have used artistic license to fill a few gaps but these accounts are closely based on actual events and the joys and sorrows of real people.

PWM 2013

---

[1]Now Foley's School Limassol

DAYS WE HAVE SEEN

Photo by Michael Michael 1973 - From the Collection of Vassos Stylianou

Famagusta beach as we knew it

The Moving Finger writes; and, having writ,
Moves on: nor all thy Piety nor Wit
Shall lure it back to cancel half a Line,
Nor all thy Tears wash out a Word of it.

The Rubáiyát of Omar Khayyám

Chapter 1 - WAR AND EVACUATION

The Patriotic Baker and the Coup d'état

July 1974 in Famagusta was extremely hot and dry. It was like that every year but this year it was different, this year we could not go to the beach to swim or even sit out in the shade of the large trees in our little garden. This year a curfew had been imposed across the country and we had been ordered to stay in our homes.

Our four year old son, Zim, had just started to master his little stabilised bike and couldn't understand why it wasn't safe to go outside and ride around and we tried to devise games to keep him happy. Floating all sorts of unlikely toys in the bathtub was a favourite, especially if we got soaking wet in the process. Feeling claustrophobic I padded around the house in bare feet with the minimum of clothing, nervously killing time, waiting to see what would develop. We were renting an old house with solid walls and a red-tiled pitched roof which was cooler than the modern concrete buildings but, even with the windows open and the slatted wooden shutters closed, it was still oppressively hot.

Being at the top of a hill a good deal of the neighbourhood was visible from our windows and I scanned the streets for any sign of life but nothing moved except the occasional military jeep passing at high speed packed with heavily armed soldiers. The only civilian I saw was a lone hippie-like character in a sleeveless tie-dyed purple vest who shot past the door at high speed on a powerful motorbike, his long hair and full beard flowing in the wind.

One of my neighbours was a baker called Antonis. Early one morning, alerted by the sound of an engine running outside, I got out of bed and peeped through the shutters that faced his house. I watched with growing anger and frustration while a scruffy bunch of irregular soldiers pushed him roughly down his garden path and into a waiting army jeep. Although early it was already hot but I suspected that the sweat that glistened on Antonis' bald head was more to do with fear than the heat. He didn't resist much, simply calling back words of encouragement to his wife, but the soldiers took every opportunity to show him, with slaps and kicks, who was in charge. Summoning up his courage Antonis pulled his thin, lanky frame up to its full height as the soldiers squeezed into the open jeep beside him and, with a grinding of gears and a cloud of dust, they roared away down the deserted street.

I learned later that Antonis's crime was to be an official of the bakers' union and as such, in the eyes of the extreme right, dangerously left wing. All over the city people like Antonis were being rounded up and thrown into prison by the supporters of EOKA-B, an extreme right wing group seeking union with Greece, which had just staged a coup d'état to overthrow the government of Cyprus. Whereas EOKA[2] in the 1950s were seen by the majority of the Greek Cypriots as anti-colonial freedom fighters, EOKA-B had the support of only a small minority of the Greek Cypriot population.

Since arriving in Cyprus in 1972 we had become familiar with the struggle between EOKA-B and the government. The original EOKA movement had fought to free Cyprus from British rule and unite the island with Greece, but this proved impractical with a large Turkish population (18%). The vast majority of Cypriots, therefore, opted for an independent state in which power was shared by Greek and Turkish Cypriots. Archbishop Makarios, a charismatic leader in the original EOKA struggle, having accepted the need for an independent state, became its first president and although the power sharing government collapsed soon after independence in 1960, he remained recognised internationally as the legitimate ruler of

---

[2]EOKA *Ethniki Organosis Kyprion Agoniston* (National Organisation of Cypriot Fighters)

the island. By 1972 those who saw Archbishop Makarios's change of direction as a betrayal had formed EOKA-B and were backed by the military dictatorship that then ruled Greece. General George Grivas, an unreconstructed hero of the original anti-colonial struggle, had secretly returned to the island the previous year and tensions between EOKA-B, supported by the Cyprus army (the National Guard, led by mainland Greek officers) and the government, supported by the police, were escalating.

In the two years between arriving in Cyprus and the coup d'état in 1974, we had become accustomed to hearing bombs exploding in the night and surveying the wrecked shops or businesses or even small police stations the next morning. Unlike in the conflict in Northern Ireland, these bombs were never targeted at people but always at property.

Our first bomb after arriving, however, was close and a real shock. The first blast shook the house and May and I woke up trembling. We sat up in bed and wondered what to do. Our neighbour's lights came on briefly and then all was dark and quiet again so I checked that Zim was still sleeping soundly and, feeling much calmer, went back to bed and settled back to sleep. Suddenly a second huge explosion shook the bed and we were again sitting up in bed holding hands with our hearts pounding. There was no attempt to sleep for a while after that; a cup of tea was made while we sat in the kitchen waiting for the next explosion which never came.

The next morning I cycled a few hundred yards up the hill to the small police station that I suspected was the target. In the heat of the summer the scene that met my eyes had an unreal quality. Everything seemed so normal, the insects clicked in the dry grass, the cicadas shrilled in the nearby carob trees but the police station had almost completely disappeared. A small group of people talked quietly as they watched a few policemen who were picking through the rubble.

A story, so prevalent at the time I am convinced it was true, soon spread about the bombing. Apparently masked gunmen entered the station and ordered the police officers out of the building. One of the officers refused to move as he had parked his brand new car nearby and knew it would be wrecked in the blast. A fierce argument ensued but the gunmen finally relented and, accompanied by his assailants, the policeman was allowed to drive his car, at gunpoint, to a safe place. This was terrorism with a human dimension and, as far-fetched as it may seem, in Cyprus that was completely plausible.

In early July 1974 Archbishop Makarios wrote to the Greek junta demanding the withdrawal of all mainland Greek officers from the army and we waited with some anxiety for the response. My family in England were anxious and letters arrived seeking reassurance that we were safe. I assured them that everything would be fine, arguing that the Greek junta would never be crazy enough to stage a coup d'état. A few days later, on 15th July, there was a coup d'état and an attempt was made to kill President Makarios. His death was widely reported in the media; but he escaped to Paphos in the far west of the island and was able to broadcast a brief message to his people before being whisked to safety by a British helicopter.

On hearing this news, despite a strict curfew imposed by the new EOKA-B 'rulers', the mass of the people came out of their houses chanting 'Makarios lives, Makarios lives'. From my front door I had a good view down the hill towards the sea and saw crowds of jubilant people of all ages jumping and waving in the streets. Fearing for their safety they soon returned to the shelter of their homes and the streets were still and quiet again after a few minutes, but that brief episode was one of the most moving spectacles I have ever seen and the memory of it still touches me.

Under the terms of the Treaty of Guarantee granted to Cyprus upon gaining independence, Britain, Greece and Turkey were obliged to intervene militarily to restore the peace and independence of the island. For one reason or another the obligations of these three guarantors were quickly put aside. Greece and its allies were actively working against the treaty in an endeavour to extend their influence over the eastern

Mediterranean and the British saw it as in their best interest to limit their response to diplomatic manoeuvring[3]. Turkey felt it had to protect the Turkish Cypriots from the new regime and had long sought a partitioning of the island along ethnic lines. Acting unilaterally it invaded the island, preferring to call its action a 'peace keeping operation'.

In later years a Cypriot friend with a good command of English would agree bitterly with this, saying that the Turks had, indeed, taken a piece of Cyprus and were now keeping it. Despite the best efforts of the international community that partition remains at the time of writing almost forty years later.

As soon as the Turkish army invaded the political prisoners were released and Antonis, like many Cypriot men a keen hunter, rushed home to get his shotgun.

Although the small National Guard force and a few irregulars armed with shotguns had little chance of stopping one of NATO's most efficient fighting machines, every able bodied Greek Cypriot was called upon to take up arms. Seeing Antonis hurrying down his garden path, gun in hand, I apprehended him at his gate and asked him where he was going.

"To fight the Turk Kyrie Petro,[4]" he panted. "Sorry not to talk now, I must to go to fight."

His battered van spluttered into life and he was gone, off to fight alongside those who had been his jailers and all that remained was a cloud of dust and the smell of black exhaust fumes. That was the last I saw of him and I didn't know until I bumped into him many years later if he had survived the war or

---

[3] A great deal has been written about the role of the British and American governments in the Coup d'état and subsequent invasion of Cyprus and I have no wish to add to it here. I would recommend 'Cyprus' by Christopher Hitchens and 'The Cyprus Conspiracy' by Brendan O'Malley and Ian Craig for further reading for those interested in power politics.

[4] Literal translation: Mr Peter

died with his feeble hunting rifle in his hands. He was a good man and he taught me that, for better or worse, patriotism can run deep in a Cypriot.

The Invasion and evacuation

We were lying, face down, under the dining room table in the middle of our friends' house. This, according to BFBS (British Forces Broadcasting Service), was the safest place to be during an air-raid and we had seen Turkish fighter jets circling high overhead a few minutes earlier. The adults and children of three families squeezed together as far under the table as we could all get, hoping the bombs would not fall too close. I thought back to our own home and hoped it would not be damaged in the bombing.

We lived on one of the highest streets in the Varosha area of Famagusta. From the front door the land dropped away to the sea and from the back a gentle slope of scattered houses and citrus orchards fell away to level ground. Good Cypriot friends living further down the hill had telephoned to warn us that the water tower close to our house might be a target and invited us to move over to their house. May and I discussed the situation at length and decided to risk breaking the curfew and take up their kind offer.

Locking the front door I paused and looked around me wondering if we were doing the right thing. There had been few jeeps in the streets since the Turkish invasion but the curfew was still in force and the walk to the safety of our friends' house would take several minutes. Zim was impatient to get going, his best friend Jason was our friends' youngest son and after being cooped up in the house for days he relished the prospect of having someone to play with. A quick look up to the water tower convinced me, we had to risk it and go. I turned the key and the three of us set off along the deserted road little knowing that it would be over a year before we would see our home again and the city of Famagusta would then look very, very different. In one hand I held a small suitcase into which May had had the presence of mind to hurriedly throw our passports and a few things for Zim and in the other Zim's hand as he skipped excitedly between us. He was happy and May was, as always, very calm but I was frightened. To protect and take good care of your family is a basic instinct and I was fearful for our safety. The sound of an approaching car startled me and in the glare of the sun I thought at first it was a military vehicle but it turned out to be dark green commercial van and my heart beat slowed again.

I decided I was far too jumpy which was not good for any of us and resigned myself for whatever was in store for us in the uncertain future. We reached the house without incident and were warmly welcomed by our friends Photis and Yana Photiou and their two sons Eas and Jason. The adults were putting on a brave face for the sake of the children but the strain they were under was clearly etched on their faces.

I became calmer but it was a frightening time. The old city of Famagusta was home to most of the Turkish Cypriots in the area and was under attack from Greek Cypriot forces. From our garden I had watched fireballs falling from the Turkish planes attacking these forces in the area around the old city; they reminded me of the pictures I had seen of napalm bombings in Vietnam. Unfortunately this area was heavily populated and many civilians fell victim to the bombs. The main hospital was also in this area and I heard later that several babies in incubators had to be left behind when the electricity was cut and the hospital evacuated.

We had been under the table for quite some time, trying to hold a cheerful conversation to keep our spirits up and to stop the children becoming frightened, when we noticed that the two four year old boys had managed to slip out without being noticed. Extremely alarmed Photis and I began a frantic search for our sons. Calling out their names we checked every room in the house but they were nowhere to be found. Bewildered, we decided to look outside and there they were, standing brazenly in the middle of the street with sticks for guns aiming at the swooping planes and making all the appropriate sound effects of gunfire and explosions. They were having great fun. The planes were some distance away but the feeling of relief as I swept Zim up in my arms was overwhelming. He is a grown man now but the feel of the warm, moist skin of his small body has stayed with me down the years and whenever I feel downhearted I remember it and thank heaven that I have him still. He couldn't understand what all the fuss was about; it seems the adults were more worried than the children.

Time passed and the bombers started to hit targets closer to us. For some time the BFBS radio station had been urging British nationals to evacuate the city in convoys protected by the British army but we were reluctant to leave, believing the fighting would be over in a few days and we would be able to return home. Eventually the radio announced that the last convoy the army were able to protect would leave that afternoon and all British nationals remaining in the city were urged to join it at an assembly point in downtown Varosha. After much discussion it was decided that Photis would stay but the rest of us would leave. Although we were reluctant to split up the family and leave Photis alone we reasoned that the SBA (Sovereign Base Area)[5] at Dhekelia was not far away and that we would be re-united again before too long. Three women (Yana's sister and her son were there too), four children and the few belongings we thought worth taking were all packed into one car with me at the wheel. I took a good look at Photis's face as we pulled slowly away from their door and it told a sad story of sleepless nights, anxious days and the pain of separation from his loved ones. He was not to see them again for months.

The hot, packed car was tense as we wove our way through the deserted streets of the city but I felt calmer than I had for days because now we were taking decisive action and

---

[5]Sovereign Base Area: Although Cyprus gained independence from the British in 1960 large tracts of land remained under British control. These military bases were considered to be vital to Britain's strategic interests.

would soon be in a safe place and not at the mercy of falling bombs. The children though, were noticeably subdued. Eas was old enough to understand something of the gravity of the situation and Jason and Zim, who had until then been full of mischief and garrulous, began to sense that something was wrong.

The convoy stood almost fully formed in the sweltering heat; a long line of cars with army trucks and Land Rovers, their roofs covered with large Union Jack flags, interspersed every so often between them. I looked up at the tall hotel buildings nearby on top of which the Cypriots had mounted anti-aircraft guns and saw people on some of the balconies. (Soon after we left these hotels were bombed and many people lost their lives. In the UK the TV newsreels showed again and again pictures of a body hanging from the ruins of one of those destroyed balconies). We joined the end of the convoy and were soon approached by a friendly British soldier. In the heat and confusion his neatly pressed uniform and confident manner were very reassuring. Our calmness soon evaporated when he told us that, although we all had British passports, because some of us were Cypriots we would not be allowed to join the convoy but would have to follow behind. No large Union Jack protection for us.

The convoy eventually set off with our car leading a line of about twenty others which also did not qualify to enjoy the protection of the British army. A fast pace was set as we dashed through the empty streets at high speed and we struggled to keep up in our small, overloaded car. We had been driving for less than five minutes when a bizarre incident, almost dreamlike in oddity, threatened our safe passage to the sanctuary of the SBA. Without warning a large black Mercedes emerged from the driveway of a house on our left and shot across the road in front of us, stopping in the middle of the road and blocking our path. I hit the brakes and came to a halt only a few feet from the driver, a large, wild eyed man wearing a stained white vest. Dripping with sweat he glared for a few moments up and down the street without seeming to register that we were there and then reversed at high speed back onto the pavement and sat staring straight ahead apparently unable to decide what to do next. The road ahead was clear and we lost no time in continuing our pursuit of the convoy but it was hopeless. In those few moments they had disappeared and we had no idea of their route.

We found our way back to the assembly point followed by all the other cars and a small crowd of worried would-be evacuees soon surrounded the few soldiers left there seeking advice. It was hot, we were anxious and tempers became frayed. We were told there was no question of any sort of protection and we would all have to make our own way to the SBA. We were shown an example of the small cardboard indicators that marked the route and told that we should hurry as another wave of bombing could happen at any time. The occupants of the other cars agreed to follow us again and we set off once more, somewhat anxious and wary as the curfew had not been officially lifted and we were worried about both bombs from overhead and EOKA- B guerrillas on the roads.

Following the small signs was not easy but we made good progress until, on the outskirts of the city, we came to a fork in the road and looked in vain for an indication of the route. I stopped the car, got out warily and searched for a fallen sign. It was eerily quiet and only the dry clicking of the insects and the rustling of the parched grass in the warm breeze broke the silence. My heightened senses picked up the hot, sticky smell of rotten fruit that came from the nearby citrus orchard and to this day that smell takes me back to that crucial fork in the road. Finding no sign I walked back to the following cars but no one had any idea about which road to take so, trusting to fate, we opted to take the left fork. To our relief this proved to be the right road and, although we occasionally saw small bands of armed men patrolling through the orchards, we eventually reached the sanctuary of the British base.

We had hoped to sit it out in Dhekelia, the army base close to Famagusta at the eastern end of the island, for a few days and return to our homes when it was safe to do so; but it soon became clear that this was not going to be possible. Greek Cypriot refugees were pouring into the safety of the base and pandemonium reigned. I was amazed; where had all these people come from? The roads had seemed deserted but here they were in their thousands. Dealing with an influx of such great numbers in an orderly fashion would have been problematic at any time but in the current situation when people were distressed and often frantic it was impossible. The British authorities were struggling to maintain order in the chaos but were overwhelmed.

We were eventually told where to park the car and made our way to a brick building where we were allocated a room in which to wait with other British passport holders to be processed. There was much pushing and shoving and jostling for attention but we were finally at the processing desk where a British officer sat coolly and professionally dealing with one group of distressed individuals after another. He was a contrast of temperatures; the outer layer, his crisply laundered uniform, still impeccable in the heat and confusion. His body though was hot and tell-tale beads of sweat stood out on his top lip and glistened on his forehead. Inside his head his brain was as unruffled and sharp as his neatly pressed shorts. He had slept in his usual bed last night and would do so again tonight, he was working in unusual circumstances but within a familiar structure, an efficient cog in a well-oiled machine. I have never wanted to join the armed forces but I think at that moment many of us, dislocated from all we found familiar, envied him his sense of place. From the lips of that officer, in the most gentlemanly fashion, I heard for the first time myself and my family referred to as refugees.

To our dismay we were told that, as British passport holders, we would be evacuated to the UK. Believing we would be able to return to our homes within a few days we put up strenuous arguments to stay in Dhekelia but it was explained to us that there was not enough food or accommodation for the thousands seeking refuge so we would be shipped out. We hated the idea but looking around us at the clamouring crowds it seemed a fair point and we agreed to be flown to Akrotiri, another SBA on the south coast far removed from the conflict, and renew our plea to stay there.

Those of us destined to be flown back to the UK were a motley bunch consisting of Cypriots with British passports, civilians of various nationalities among whom were several stranded tourists. One of the tourists stands out in my mind as she had incredibly long finger nails that hung down in rattling spirals. I saw her again a few days later on TV being interviewed about her ordeal.

For the short flight to Akrotiri we were packed into a troop-carrying Hercules. These aircraft were not designed to carry civilian passengers. A row of back to back seats was fitted down the length of the fuselage and two further rows were fitted along the lengths of the sides. May and I strapped ourselves into two of the middle seats facing Yana and her boys seated with their backs to the opposite side. I held Zim on my lap and answered his non-stop questions about everything he could see around him. Fortunately he never asked about the hole in the wall that was a toilet suitable for men only.

The Hercules is a large four engine propeller aircraft with the wings above the fuselage and it is not built for comfort. The sound of the engines, which hang below the wings at the same level as the cabin, as it warmed up was deafening. It stood in the heat vibrating madly as the noise built to a crescendo and we thought the thing was going to shake itself to pieces but then brakes were released and we were off, hurtling wildly down the short dirt runway. The bumps from the undercarriage now added to the shaking and we all breathed a sigh of relief as we miraculously shot smoothly off a low cliff and were above the sparkling blue of the Mediterranean. Our brief moment of tranquillity was interrupted by a sharp banking turn to the right and I found myself looking straight down to the sea below. Fortunately I had my arms around Zim and I tightened my grip on him then to prevent him falling across the cabin but we soon levelled out and the rest of the short journey west was uneventful, if somewhat noisy. I heard later that friends had been flown in short hops all the way home to the UK in Hercules aircraft, which must have been extremely uncomfortable.

Akrotiri was a little less chaotic than Dhekelia and as we walked into the processing area my hopes rose a little. The officer who handled us here was not as sympathetic as his counterpart in Dhekelia and gave us the stark choice of either getting on a 'plane to the UK or being taken to the edge of the SBA and left there to fend for ourselves. This seemed to us at the time to be a tough line to take but in retrospect we understood that, as in Dhekelia, the authorities were overwhelmed by thousands of refugees and were short of food and bedding so it was right to send those of us who were entitled back to the UK. We had been reluctant to leave our home from the beginning and still believed we would be able to go back there in a few days so the forced expulsion to England, thousands of miles away, was very hard to take and we resolved to return as soon as possible.

Tired and depressed we settled down to wait for our flight and soon met a number of old friends from Famagusta who were in much worse shape than us. I remember particularly the wife of a doctor who had last seen her husband several days before heading for the hospital that she had heard since had been bombed. Somehow the plight of others gave us the strength to forget our minor worries and try to support them.

Eventually we got the call to board and we carried the sleeping children into the aircraft. No ramshackle propeller 'plane this time and soon we were high in the air in the luxury of a Royal Air Force Boeing 747 with all the trappings of a commercial flight including cabin crew and refreshments. I had always been a nervous flyer but after the risks of the previous few days nothing seemed very dangerous and I soon fell asleep and slept for most of the flight.

After a few hours we found ourselves landing at a place we had never heard of. Brize Norton was the largest RAF base in the country but we were ignorant of it and had no idea where in the country it was located. Fortunately the weather was kind to us and we did not feel too cold in the flimsy clothes we were wearing and, with a very welcome lack of delay, we were loaded onto a red double-decker bus bound for London. The children, who had recovered a little now, scrambled up the stairs to the upper deck to get 'Good views of England'. I expected a short journey but we had the delight of over sixty miles of England in all her glory.

After the burnt landscape of Cyprus the drive through the lush green Oxfordshire countryside seemed like heaven. Huge green oak trees lined the country lanes and their leaves brushed the windows of the upper deck where we sat. The rolling, verdant meadows and fields of wheat, almost ready to harvest, seemed like a safe and beautiful other world; a world I had known and loved as a child growing up in rural Norfolk.

Although I was thankful that we were safe, I could not feel content. Cyprus had been good to us and it felt as though we were leaving her in times of trouble. Deep inside I felt a simmering resentment that we had been forced to leave behind so many good friends whose fate we did not know. We had many Turkish Cypriot friends living in the old Venetian walled city of Famagusta which we knew was being bombarded and didn't know if they were alive or dead. Our home in the Varosha district of Famagusta filled with so many fond memories now seemed very far away and I pictured it in my mind, trying to remember it clearly, suspecting for the first time that we might have lost it for a while. Sitting on that London bus with the green fields of England sliding by May and I vowed to return to Cyprus as soon as possible.

Chapter 2 - ENGLAND

Our families welcomed us back with open arms and great relief; they had watched the Cyprus drama unfold on television and had feared for our safety. We stayed in London with May's brother, Naysan, and his family for a few days before going up to my family in North Norfolk.

My parents' hospitality knew no bounds and we stayed with them for a while enjoying the tranquillity of a rural life. With my father we enjoyed pleasant walks in the nearby woods and visits to the beach, both filled with boyhood memories that gave those outings a special poignancy. My mother cared for us as only mothers can and to taste her home-cooked meals again was wonderful. For the first time in his life Zim could enjoy the company and affection of his grandparents and he soon came to love the quiet, deeply felt, affection they showed him.

Life on one level was very comfortable but we realised that we could not go on living at my parents' expense indefinitely and, with local job prospects almost non-existent, we would have to move if we were to find work.

We decided to return to London where May's brother worked in the West End as a graphic designer and we both found work quite quickly. May had excellent typing skills and had no trouble in finding work with the many local temping agencies until, with Naysan's help, I secured a highly paid post with a public relations company co-ordinating an extensive graphic design project producing illustrative slides for a major oil company.

Our lives had taken another dramatic turn. From a small seaside city in scorching Cyprus we had gone to the peaceful rural idyll of North Norfolk and now we found ourselves caught up in the high pressure world of big business in the heart of one of the biggest cities in the world. I enjoyed it. The hours were long and the pressures were real but the work was creative and stimulating. The company that employed me was owned by a Bahá'í and had an unerring ethical compass that guided everything we did.

Life with Naysan, his wife Zohreh and their little three year old daughter, Chereh, was hugely enjoyable. Naysan and I worked in the same office and shared the same sense of humour which made the long hours pass quickly and when we went home our two families were like one family. We would often wonder as we rattled homeward on the underground what new pranks Zim and Chereh had been up to that day. Always a little crazy, there was something about his cousin's company that made Zim anarchic. Chereh in her turn, inspired by his madness, would devise schemes that eclipsed even his daring. Often the most challenging task of our day was trying not to laugh as we reprimanded them for their latest escapade.

Life was good, my salary was beyond the dreams of an art teacher and, after a very successful conclusion to the slide project I was offered a permanent post. Long before the days of PowerPoint we had devised a way of illustrating presentations using 35mm slides on multiple projectors and Jerry, the company owner, wanted to create a new company to specialise in this work.

'Stay for two or three years,' he said. 'You will make enough money to go back to Cyprus and live very comfortably instead of going back and living like a refugee'.

I turned his offer down saying that the money was a golden cage in which everyone in the business sat and would never escape.

'I intend to get out of this business in five years from now and go to live on an island in the Pacific.' he replied, 'The money will not trap me so it need not trap you'.

I told him that I doubted he would ever do it but was delighted to hear a few years later that he had moved to Samoa.

Once again Cyprus was calling us in a way I have found difficult to explain to bewildered family and friends. There was something about the island that made us feel we belonged there and our sense of dislocation, even after months away, was palpable. We started to make plans to return.

We had enough saved to cover the fares back to Cyprus and pay our living expenses for about a year. Communications were not so easy in those days but I learned on the grapevine that the school in which I had taught in Famagusta had tentatively re-opened with a few pupils in Limassol on the south coast and that there was a chance of a little work there.

Zim 1975

Chapter 3 - RETURN TO CYPRUS

The journey

We set off in early November 1974 with two rucksacks containing all our possessions; these seemed rather a lot at the time as we had arrived with practically nothing. Zim proudly carried his own little rucksack full of his 'special things'. We also had an old post office bag full of clothes which our friends and relatives had donated for the refugees. Bidding farewell to our worried families was extremely difficult.

Nicosia airport had been destroyed and there were no commercial flights to the island so we travelled overland. To cut costs we had not booked sleeping accommodation on the trains that would take us from London to Athens so we slept as best we could sitting up when the train was crowded or stretched out on the seats when there was enough room.

Lying awake as the train clattered through France to Italy, I had time for reflection and memories of my family as we said goodbye came back to me vividly. Some had covered their feelings better than others but the anxious faces of my parents and sister still haunted me. Was I right I wondered, to set off on another adventure when they had already had so many worries about me down the years. At the age of thirty and married with a young child should I have settled for a life more ordinary? 'Quo Vadis?' I asked myself, 'Where are you going?' The answer was that I was following my heart; that I felt there was a 'rightness' about what I was doing that was unshakeable. Maybe I was making a big mistake but I had to do what I felt, deep down, was right.

When we changed trains in Venice the standard of our compartment changed for the worse but the journey was reasonably comfortable until we reached what was then

Yugoslavia. Soon the train began to fill with Greeks with left wing convictions who had fled to Eastern Bloc countries during the extreme right wing dictatorship in their own. The military junta in Greece had now collapsed following the fiasco in Cyprus and these people were on their way home to vote in the first democratic election for years.

In our compartment we took turns to sit Zim on our laps to free up another seat but soon even the space between the seats was packed with standing people. As we rattled down the length of the country the train filled little by little until it was bursting at the seams. Using the toilet became almost impossible; just getting there was a fight through corridors crammed with passengers and the sight and smell that greeted us made us wonder if we really should have bothered.

Conditions became intolerable and some of us elected to use the first class carriages which were scarcely occupied. Here we felt we would get the accommodation we had paid for and, for a while, we had a degree of comfort but it did not last long. Soon the whole train was heaving with bodies but the atmosphere was festive. The people were squashed and tired, the air was stuffy and the stench was awful but they were happy to be returning to their homeland to vote.

Athens was buzzing with excited expectation. The sense of a people emerging from repression was tangible and although we were exhausted from the long journey our spirits could not help but be buoyed up by the atmosphere in the railway station, the streets and the cafes. Our fellow passengers fell into the arms of their relatives and friends with relief and joy. Tears flowed, backs were slapped, elderly mothers in black clasped their sons to them as though they would never let them go. A weeping grandmother, almost too feeble to stand unaided, stood staring at her grandson hardly able to believe her eyes. Maybe she had prayed that she would live long enough to see his return and stood dumbfounded as he said gently,

'Yaya mou, ti ganeteh?' (My granny, how are you?').

After a brief stop-over with friends in Athens we made our way to the port of Piraeus and found the ferry from

Cyprus. People were still leaving the island in droves and we waited patiently while the incoming boat disgorged crowds of people. Once on board we realised that very few people were making the return journey and we delighted in the luxury of almost unlimited space after our days of cramped confinement. Breathing the fresh air on the sunlit deck was wonderful after the stuffiness of the train and the pollution in Athens.

We watched preparations for departure. The pitch of the engine rose. With shouts mooring ropes were slipped from quayside bollards, splashed into the water and were winched on board. Slowly, slowly we moved away from the jetty. The feeling that I was being released from a confinement of sorts came over me as the eddying waters between the boat and land grew wider and wider. Soon the land was a speck behind us, the wind was tugging my hair, a salty tang hung in the air and we were ploughing through the open sea.

We were travelling steerage and went below to our separate cabins. Meeting up again on deck May reported that she had the female dormitory cabin to herself and Zim and I could tell her that we shared the male dormitory with just one young man. Those were happy days, chugging slowly through the Greek islands with the whole boat to roam around in. We had an early scare when Zim, who liked nothing better than to go off on his own to talk to whoever would listen to him, went missing for a while. We were frantic but found him chatting to a young couple who were trying to find out where he was from in Greek. After that we set up a system whereby whichever of us that had possession of a distinctive comb, handed over with great ceremony, had the responsibility of keeping an eye on our thrill-seeking son.

The young man who shared our dormitory got off the boat in Rhodes and, as we now had the cabin to ourselves, May moved in with Zim and me.

Up on the rusty old deck in the weak sunshine during the day or lying awake in the dark listening to the regular thud of the engines at night, each turn of those engines taking us closer to Cyprus, I felt a growing sense of excitement. I had little idea what lay ahead, but I knew it would be an adventure.

Cyprus

As our boat slowly nosed into Limassol harbour and tied up at the quayside I reflected on the fact that we were arriving in a town that we didn't know at all. But we had friends here who, like us, were refugees from Famagusta. Quentin had taught with me at the Famagusta Grammar School and his wife Nikki taught English at one of the Famagusta Gymnasiums[6]. We hauled on our rucksacks and dragged our old post office bag off the boat and into the deserted customs hall where the startled customs officials could hardly believe their eyes. As everyone who could do so was leaving they could not understand why we British nationals had come back. We tried to explain that we felt Cyprus was our home but they shook their heads in disbelief as they stamped our passports clearly of the opinion that we were crazy. The informal and friendly way they went about their business, calling Zim a 'clever monkey' because he carried his own rucksack and smiling and joking with us, confirmed to me that, whilst we might well be crazy, the decision to return was a good one.

We found our way to our friends' apartment in a modern block fairly close to the town centre. With them in their small apartment they already had their small baby and had the care of Nikki's parents who had an apartment in the same block but they insisted we stay with them until we could find a place of our own.

From Quentin and Nikki and the local media we learned the realities of the circumstances into which we had placed ourselves. The situation in Cyprus was desperate. The economy was in ruins; the Turkish army now controlled about 40% of the island and virtually all the tourist accommodation and citrus

---

[6]Gymnasium: academic secondary school

production. The government of Cyprus estimated that the country was losing some $4.5 million in economic production every day. People were still trying to trace family members and friends who had been lost in the chaos of war and over 1,600 individuals were classified as missing[7]. Of a population of approximately half a million, 200,000 were now refugees. In September 1974 the Service for the Care and Rehabilitation for Displaced Persons (ΥΜΑΠΕ) was established to deal with the situation but the authorities were struggling to cope.

Fortunately, Cypriots are, by and large, industrious and hard-working and efficient systems were already in place to distribute food and clothing and to find accommodation for those still homeless. Many refugees found shelter in houses that had been evacuated by the British forces or in unfinished buildings or in schools.

In Limassol offices had been set up in empty houses and business premises and although these were always noisy and crowded the government employees and volunteers who worked there were doing a good job in difficult circumstances. It was sobering to see men drive to these offices in the large expensive cars that they had managed to bring south with them and then queue for hours for a voucher with which to buy a pair of shoes.

We did not wish to add to the burden on the authorities but were persuaded by our friends to register ourselves as refugees and, on a dull and surprisingly cold morning, made our way to one of the hastily formed offices in the rooms of an old house. The building was already crowded and we struggled with our limited Greek to find our way to the appropriate room but our fellow refugees were invariably kind and helpful and as we queued I felt a strong sense of kinship with them. We did not consider ourselves to be the same as the other refugees as we had voluntarily returned to the country but we had been thrown out of our home and lost everything and I felt we were

---

[7] Many of these missing persons have disappeared without trace and it seems unlikely that their fate will ever be known

back among people like us. Looking at their faces, some anxious, some stoic, some tearful, I wondered where they were from and what stories they could tell; who and what had they lost in that brief, one sided conflict. We had returned with the intention of helping the refugees and this first visit to a relief centre strengthened our resolve to volunteer.

We were unsure about the reception we would receive as we were not Cypriots but when we arrived at the processing desk the officials didn't hesitate in issuing us with identity cards and books in which to record the provisions and articles with which we would be supplied. Half expecting rejection we tentatively offered to help in any way we could. Quite what two, virtually non-Greek speaking foreigners could do we didn't know but our offer was graciously received and we were asked to return a few days later. Maybe, we thought, they are letting us down gently and when we go back they will say they can find nothing for us to do. We underestimated them. Before long we were sitting with a remarkable woman, who I only remember as Kyria[8] Dora, as she explained what she had in mind for us.

---

[8]Mrs in Greek

Chapter 4 - THE SCHOOL

A volunteer herself, Kyria Dora, briefed us on the situation in a large primary school in the centre of Limassol where scores of refugees had been housed. The school still functioned on the ground and second floor of the three storey building with the refugees housed in the classrooms sandwiched between them on the first floor. Tensions within this little community had risen to breaking point. The women still had, to a degree, their traditional roles of cooks and housewives but the men had nothing to do and time weighed heavily on them. It was almost impossible to find employment in the devastated economy and fruitless searches for work caused despair and anger. Frustrated with their situation they had become quarrelsome and the occasional fight had broken out. In one incident a father with learning difficulties had beaten his wife. Kyria Dora felt that May could help by setting up English and handicraft classes for the children and that I should work with the wife beater, Christos, to help him make a bed for his children.

With some reservations we accompanied Kyria Dora to the school and were pleased to be given a cautious welcome. I had never seen myself as a social worker but it soon became obvious that we were accepted as individuals no matter what the refugees thought of our government and most seemed to find our presence heartening.

Christos

Christos was unusually tall and powerfully built with light brown hair and clear blue-grey eyes. We were introduced and he accepted the hand of friendship I offered him, crushing it in his outsized fist. We got down to work and he seemed to understand most of my broken Greek and sign language as we started work together on the construction of the bed. This was not a simple task as there was very little money available for even basic requirements like wood or tools and I remembered wistfully the huge amounts of money I had had at my disposal a few weeks earlier on the oil company project in London. Christos had 'borrowed' several pieces of broad wooden shuttering from a building site and together we scraped off the cement and started to split them into narrower pieces.

Whenever I hear the expression 'Not the sharpest tool in the box' I think of Christos and the one good tool we had at our disposal. It was a large sharp axe that he had found somewhere and I held the timber while he split it. I was very nervous at first; he was clearly not too intelligent and was prone to outbreaks of violence, but as the days passed I came to realise that my fears were unfounded and grew to admire his simple determination to make life a little more comfortable for his family. I was never sure how he felt about me but I will always think of him as a friend.

We settle into a routine

May's classes with the children were a great success. In an open communal area she set up tables and soon had the children, and sometimes the adults, drawing and painting and making simple handicrafts. I bought a few simple tools and was able to make learning aids and games from waste materials. Grocery shops were a favourite source of cardboard, wire, hardboard, string and other excellent packaging materials. The local grocers would keep these various bits and pieces that they knew I would find useful set aside for me. The children were also enthusiastic to learn English which May wove unobtrusively into the activities. A pattern soon emerged where she would teach classes whilst I helped individuals with various projects or played football with the younger people in the school playground.

Playing football was easy but some of the conversations with the youth were extremely difficult. They were proud and thin-skinned and found it difficult to accept that the Turks had beaten them in a very one-sided war.

'One Greek is worth ten Turks.' they would say. 'A Greek heart is more stronger than a Turkish heart. We will throw them into the sea'.

One boy quoted Winston Churchill's famous speech in which he said that instead of saying "Greeks fight like heroes." we must now say, "Heroes fight like Greeks." I could understand their bravado but it saddened me. A heart, no matter how strong, is no match for a bullet and the prospect of the Cypriot National Guard defeating the might of the Turkish army was a fantasy. Those boys were still being fed propaganda that encouraged the notion of armed conflict as their duty and only option. I had to be extremely careful in any discussions I had with them (and others) as all foreigners, particularly the British and Americans, were viewed with suspicion.

It was obvious to us all that the superpowers would have their agents in place (in later years it was a game with some of my friends at expatriate gatherings to try to guess who the spies might be) and I did not want to become suspected of being one of them. We had, after all, returned to Cyprus when more rational people were struggling to leave which was in itself suspicious. It was difficult not to challenge those fine young men determined to fight at the earliest opportunity, but I bit my tongue.

Workshop plans

When the men in the school went along to the children's classes and played with the jigsaws and other puzzles I had made for the children it became obvious that they were desperate for something to occupy their hands and minds. Life was hard for these proud men who had lost their homes and jobs and, for some, their loved ones, but not their dignity. I decided I had to start workshops in which the men could make simple artefacts that we might be able to sell.

Outlining my plans to Kyria Dora I learned that a new refugee camp was under construction at Kolossi, a small village on the Paphos road to the west and she suggested that it would be better to start a workshop there. A meeting was arranged with Kyrios[9] Stelios, the designated manager of the camp, and he liked my ideas for the handicrafts we might produce there. He told me that a workshop was already planned and asked me to produce a few examples of what could be made in order to convince the authorities that my projects were viable. In Famagusta I had supplemented my income from teaching by making various items for the tourist gift shops including novelty candles that looked just like oranges, lemons and grapefruit and I set about making samples in a small basement room which the headmaster of the school had kindly given me permission to use.

That little room, not much more than a broom cupboard, became the centre of my world for the next few weeks. Plaster of Paris, paraffin wax, gas bottles, cookers, old saucepans and citrus fruit all vied for space within its walls and there were times when I had little elbowroom to work. But the candles were soon ready and I was pleased with the colourful display they made. I felt that I was really getting somewhere when, having taken my samples away, Kyrios Stelios returned to say that I had been invited to help with the setting up of workshops when the new camp opened. Another phase of our lives as refugees had begun.

*

---

[9] Mr in Greek

Here is my account of an incident that happened early on in our days at the school

Kyriacos and the knife

Nearly everyone had gone to the kitchen to collect their lunch and the rooms of the school in which the refugees had been housed were deserted. It was November and the thin sunlight that broke through the dirty windows did little to take the chill off the air of the barren classrooms so recently stripped of their furniture.

No-one came or went. I was the only one who moved, walking softly from room to room, absorbing the mood of the place. The war had broken over the occupants of these rooms like a giant wave, throwing their settled lives into confusion and scattering them into strange and distant places, far from their village homes. They had brought with them what few things they could carry and these were washed up here, the flotsam and jetsam of a tragic conflict. Here, high and dry on the cold tile floors, lay everything they now possessed. Scattered between the bedding were crumpled cardboard boxes, ancient cheap suitcases and bundles tied up in sheets or blankets. Small bits and pieces in constant use were arranged neatly into little groups as the women struggled to bring some sort of order into the chaos of their lives.

Despina was very fat with large, wet, empty eyes and oily pitted skin and she lay fully clothed on her bedding in one of the rooms, her face against the wall. Her body rose and fell slightly with each breath and every now and then she would breathe more deeply and hold it for a few seconds before releasing it with a low sigh. I knew she was awake, staring at the wall. I called to her softly but her body just stiffened for a few moments and then returned to its old rhythm. In all the time I spent with the refugees I never saw her move from her makeshift bed. She was another piece of flotsam; wrecked and beyond my power to help and only nineteen years old. I left her alone.

Although no-one was there the next room spoke eloquently of its occupants. Three old wooden chairs and a ramshackle camp-bed had been gleaned from somewhere and a fishing net lay in the corner. (I knew a youthful member of this family who snorkelled with the net to catch fish which he sold. As he had only the top of an old wetsuit he would tie a rope tightly around his waist to ease the pain of limbs too long in cold water). The faded school posters and pictures which littered the walls of most of the classrooms had been taken down and political and religious posters put up in their place. Henry Kissinger's inane grin leered across the room at me, both sinister and comical. 'Wanted Dead or Alive' the caption read, '£1 Reward'. Above Kissinger hung a paper icon of St John the Theologian, neither sinister nor comical but with a face that radiated an infinite compassion.

I left the room in the care of the benign icon and moved on to investigate the muffled sounds coming from next door. A softly growling voice was muttering curses to the devil with little venom but with a doggedness that was unnerving. I leaned cautiously into the room and saw a very old man hunched over with his back toward me. He was sitting on a bed made up of a few blankets spread on the low dais that had once supported the teacher's desk. Moving further into the room I saw with horror what he was doing. He was hacking at his toes with a large knife and dark red blobs of blood covered the grey stone tiles under his feet.

For several moments I stood mesmerised and then I moved fast and instinctively. I dashed across the room and clamped his pulpy old wrist with one hand and grabbed the knife with the other. Both of us were so shocked that we stared at one another in disbelief for a moment which seemed to last forever.

His heavy body was cocooned in several layers of clothing and it remained bent with only the head turned to look up at me. A paunchy weathered face that had once been leathery was now sagging and grey and peppered with a bristly white stubble. Beads of sweat stood out on his forehead and glistened among the sparse hairs that covered the dome of his skull. His eyes squinted at me through the wet white mist of cataracts, he was half blind.

It was not easy for the refugees to bathe and he stank. The smell of him told of years spent under a relentless sun; of brown wax candles melting at the altars of country churches; of countless goats heaving their slimy offspring into life on lush spring hillsides; of fetid cheese and black olive juices wiped from the mouth with the back of a hand or a worn sleeve.

Our astonished silence broke into a tumble of words as I struggled with my poor Greek and he with his indignation.

'Why you do like this Mister?' I asked.

'Who the devil are you?' he fumed.

'Why you are cut your feets like this?'

'Where did you come from? Give me back my knife.'

'The feets has blood. Look, the floor has many bloods.'

'Give me my knife.'

I gave him his knife and we both calmed down. I told him who I was and he showed no surprise to find an Englishman there in his room. After all the world had gone crazy, everything was upside down, how was he supposed to make sense of it. He told me his name was Kyriacos and that he was from a village in the north. He panted as he spoke, drawing in his breath in little gasps and I was sorry to ask him to repeat things that I didn't understand.

'I can't see very well anymore and since the Turk hit me I can't bend down far enough to see my toes properly.'

'A Turk soldier, he hit you?'

'Yes. I couldn't move fast enough so he hit me in the back with his rifle.'

This was said in such a matter-of-fact way that I doubted the truth of it. The Turks tended to get the blame for everything.

'Look, look here.'

He clawed at his clothing for some time, eventually exposing the small of his back. How and when it was done I do not know but it was the most horrifying and beautiful bruise I have ever seen. Deep angry purples, violets, maroons, soft blue-greys, delicate pale yellows, blues and mauves covered the ivory flesh of the old man's back. Unbelievably beautiful as it was I could not look at it for more than a few moments.

'My toenails need cutting, I can't get my feet comfortable in my boots. What can I do? We have no scissors here so I have to use the knife.'

'But why to use such a too sharp knife Mister Kyriacos? This knife is too much dangerous.'

'It has to be sharp. Do you want me to try to do it with a knife that is blunt?'

Defeated by his logic I looked at his feet. Everything considered he had done a good job. The horny old nails had been roughly hewn into shape with only occasional slices into the flesh where the blood now congealed. The remaining uncut nails were certainly long and ugly and needed cutting. I remembered my wife had a pair of nail clippers and he agreed to try them if I brought them to him.

We were cleaning up when his wife shuffled into the room with a plate of beans for him. Her left cheek was a deep red-purple; apparently she could not move fast enough either. She scolded him at first but soon sank into a ritualistic muttering, defeated, like me, by his logic and innate anarchy. He broke a chunk off a loaf of bread and dipped it into his beans.

'She was beautiful years ago, very beautiful.'

He spoke as he chewed and managed a sly grin.

'We had nine children and six of them lived but they have all gone away. One of my sons is a doctor in Australia; another a teacher, he's in America.'

Anyone who has spoken to elderly villagers in Cyprus is familiar with the story. The parents are peasant farmers, scarcely leaving their villages. Their children are often in professions and scattered throughout the world.

I left Kyriacos and his wife enjoying their meal on the teacher's dais and returned later to clip his nails for him. They left the school unexpectedly a few weeks later and I never saw them again. But often when I cut my nails I remember that knife, those bruises and that courageous old couple.

Chapter 5 - KOLOSSI CAMP

After arriving in Cyprus we had stayed a few weeks with our friends and then moved into a small rented apartment but when my project was accepted we decided we would be of more use if we moved into the camp and lived with the rest of the refugees.

The camp at Kolossi was built on slightly undulating fields on the eastern edge of the village. Unlike the camps closer to the Green Line[10] which had been hastily thrown together to cope with the immediate aftermath of the war, Kolossi was carefully planned and well-constructed. The white canvas tents in which we lived and the large communal khaki marquees were all set on concrete bases, as were the several corrugated iron structures that housed toilets, showers and washrooms. Closer to the road stood two whitewashed concrete block buildings one housing the kitchen and the other the camp office and storerooms.

The camp looked quite pretty the first time I saw it that winter. Hundreds of white tents gleamed in the sun, billowing and flapping gently in a slight breeze. The rains had brought the dry earth to life; greenery sprouted everywhere and small wild flowers speckled the ground with bright splashes of colour. A few straggly carob trees broke the monotony of the ranks of white canvas giving what would become precious shade to adjacent tents.

---

[10]The line dividing the land controlled by the government of Cyprus from that captured by the Turkish army.

Small wild flowers speckled the ground

K. Panayides and family with May and Zim

One bright chilly morning soon after Christmas we arrived at the camp office with our now growing collection of bits and pieces. I wondered what lay in store for us as I surveyed the ranks of tents, many of them still unoccupied, and watched the few inhabitants as they went about their business. It was sunny but a feeling of desolation lurked just beneath the surface.

Zim seemed oblivious to this as he ran around exploring the facilities and enjoying the freedom that was to be a feature of his life here. As he suffered from asthma and was prone to chest problems we were offered accommodation in a little room in the building that housed the camp office and storerooms. It was tiny but we had enough room for the campbeds with which we were issued and the luxury of an adjoining toilet with a small sink and we were soon relatively comfortable. I have always enjoyed camping and, although we were not yet under canvas, I enjoyed having the fields just outside our door and the sound of the rain on the corrugated iron roof. The noise of the rain, torrential at times that winter, would often make having a conversation impossible and May and I would sit grinning at each other until the worst of the storm had passed and we could resume our talk.

Our family at the door to our room

Little by little the camp filled with refugees and a community began to form. In the early days we would collect our food from the communal kitchen and take it to one of the marquees set up with long tables and benches as dining areas. Settling down to eat cheek by jowl with each other we quickly got to know the names and circumstances of many families and, being the only foreigners in the camp, they soon got to know us.

Zim and fellow urchins at the door of the communal kitchen. He still looks like this when not wanting to be photographed

May resumed the English and handicraft classes she had begun in the school and these proved popular with the adolescents as well as the older children. We were readily accepted just as we had been at the school.

Zim enjoying the freedom of life on the camp

The large marquees had a number of uses. Two were used for dining, one was consecrated as a church, one was a kindergarten, another housed a large television and we attempted to set up a workshop in another. In the first few months the dining marquees were in constant use but as time passed we all got into the habit of taking our food back to our tents where we had gathered a few extra ingredients to make the food more interesting.

The kindergarten under canvas

After a while a group of young volunteers from Austria arrived and built two large corrugated iron sheds, one of which became our new workshop and the other the new kindergarten. As a result several of the marquees stood empty and abandoned, their guy ropes slack and their roofs sagging. Nothing goes to waste on a refugee camp and over the course of a few months these excellent sources of materials were gradually cannibalised.

A great deal of money had been spent to set up the camp and the authorities were anxious to move those still housed in schools and temporary camps into the relative comfort of Kolossi. Attempts were made to bring refugees from those schools and the hastily thrown up camps near the Green line but the desire to return to their villages was so strong that most refused to move. Although squalid, those improvised camps were closer to their homes and Kolossi was many miles to the south. Buses brought a few to see how life would be in Kolossi and we even visited camps near the Green Line to persuade people to move out but to no avail. The pull of their homes was too strong and they felt that in some way to move away would be to give up hope of ever returning.

Acceptance

Our acceptance was never more profoundly demonstrated than when, a few months later, a young Cypriot was accidentally killed whilst protesting outside the gates of the Akrotiri airbase. The western British bases had been a sanctuary for Turkish Cypriots since the first days of the coup d'état and the invasion. The Greek Cypriots were protesting against the British decision to airlift these people to the north where they would be moved into the homes the refugees had been forced to abandon.

'Greek Blood Spilled by British Armour' screamed the headlines in the tabloid press. Mass rallies were held in the streets of the major cities and I should probably have stayed on the camp for my own safety as feelings were running very high. However, a meeting for British expatriates to show support for the Government of Cyprus and to register objection to the British decision was to be held in Nicosia and I decided to go.

Worried for my safety, an official of the camp wrote a note in bold red lettering, signed and stamped it with government stamp. Translated it said: **'Attention. Please do not molest the carrier of this note Mr Peter Moore as he is an English citizen refugee from Famagusta and lives and works in the Refugee Camp of Kolossi.'** I could not imagine that to hold this note up to a mob intent on attacking me would be much of a defence but the kindness of the thought touched me and I still have that note today.

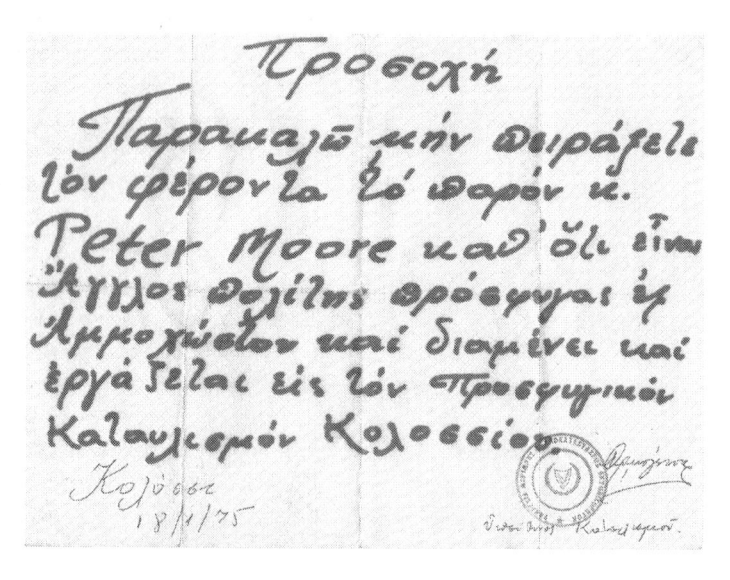

> Προσοχή
> Παρακαλώ μήν θειράζετε
> τόν φέροντα τό δώρον κ.
> Peter Moore καθ' ότι είναι
> Άγγλος Φοιτητής πρόσφυγας ἐξ
> Ἀμμοχώστου καί διαμένει καί
> ἐργάζεται εἰς τόν Προσφυγικόν
> Καταυλισμόν Κολοσσίου
> Κολοσσι
> 18/1/75

My 'Do not molest Mr Peter Moore' document

May supported me in my decision to go but it was another anxious departure as I said goodbye to her and Zim and made my way to the main road to flag down one of the service (shared) taxis that plied the roads between the major towns. These stretched Mercedes could hold up to eight passengers and were usually booked in advance but would pick up casual passengers if they had space and were excellent value for money. After a short wait I was picked up and as we headed at breakneck speed for Limassol I answered the, by now, familiar questions from the bemused driver and passengers about why I, an Englishman, was living on a refugee camp.

Near the centre of the town we were held up by a long procession of marching gymnasium pupils so I got out to join the crowds lining the streets, hoping that my tanned complexion would enable me to blend in with the crowd. The procession was led by what I believe were bereaved relatives, their eyes downcast their anguish clearly written on their faces. I remembered the faces of my own parents when we had said goodbye and my heart went out to those silent, black-clad walkers. These people were not marching or shouting, they were mourning the loss of their loved one: a young son with all his life before him who had left for school as usual one morning and came home in a coffin.

They were accompanied by local dignitaries and behind them came the chanting students and the level of noise and anger grew steadily. When I had first joined the crowds I had felt very anxious, looking nervously about me for any sign of hostility. I was aware that in this town cars that bore Union Jack stickers, put there by their owners at the time of the war for their protection, had been attacked and at least one had been turned over. As time passed I started to relax and feel quite safe but then, in the column marching towards me shouting anti-British slogans, I suddenly spotted a young man that I knew. We had played football together in the playground of the school that held the refugees. Alarmed that my nationality would be exposed I turned aside and looked down at the ground but it was no good.

"Mr Peter, how are you?" He shouted, running over to me and shaking my hand. Glancing nervously around me I had a brief, very conventional, conversation with him in English about my health, his health and the health of his mother, who had been a cleaner at the school. He then excused himself saying that he had to go and protest against the British and I made my way swiftly back to the taxi. I never knew if he ever saw the irony of what happened that day but I have always admired his complete lack of prejudice.

The meeting was no more than a gesture but we registered disapproval of our government's policy and I felt that, as little and as futile as it was, I had done what had to be done. The rest of my journey passed without incident and I was soon back with my family in the safety of the camp. Lying awake that night, listening to the familiar quiet sounds of the camp around me, I thought how strange it was that my safe haven in these troubled anti-British times was in a refugee camp full of people who felt my country had betrayed them.

*

What follows is my memory of a conversation I had with the camp carpenter during these times.

Andreas Pelecanos

Andreas Pelecanos[11] came and sat down beside me on the wooden bench next to the kafenion[12]. My spirits were low and I would rather have been alone but I liked him and enjoyed his quietly spoken broken English. He offered to buy me a coffee but my stomach was already suffering from too much of it and I knew I could decline without offending him.

It was a bad time to be an Englishman. The Callaghan government were flying the Turkish Cypriot refugees, who had fled to the British bases in the south for safety at the time of the coup d'état, to the north where the Greek Cypriot refugees knew they would eventually be moved into their homes. The Cypriot government had strongly opposed any movement of Turks from the south as this strengthened the likelihood of a physically and politically divided nation. From the camp my fellow refugees had watched the aircraft taking off from Akrotiri air base and many of them had wept at the sight. In their anxiety to show me that they made a clear distinction between me and my government I had been plied with offers of coffee for days.

Andreas settled himself onto the bench and lit a cigarette.

'Don't to worry Kyrie Petro,' he said. 'In the war many bad thing happen.'

---

[11]Pelecanos: carpenter

[12] Coffee shop

'I know," I said, 'but my country was supposed to be a guarantor power of the independence of Cyprus and they did nothing when the coup happened or when the Turks invaded except shelter the refugees on both sides. Now they've done this, which goes directly against what they were obliged to do as a guarantor power.'

'The political peoples do what they have to do Kyrie Petro, every country the same. They think for their people only and in a war peoples do bad things.'

I looked at him sideways, he had the honest, poised demeanour of a craftsman and we called him Andreas Pelecanos (the carpenter) to distinguish him from Andreas Kafeneon (the coffee shop) or Andreas Kelis (the head, baldy). He took a stick from the ground and started to trace random patterns in the dust at our feet.

'I tell you about what happen to me before Cyprus is free country when British have us in his empire.'

He took a long pull on his cigarette, and exhaled and, still scribbling in the dust, told me the following story.

'It was in the 1950s and the British were fighting against the EOKA people who wanted to unite Cyprus with Greece. It was different then you understand, we later realised that we couldn't have that, not with so many Turkish Cypriots, but then we wanted to get the British out and unite with Greece.

'We lived in Famagusta and one night my friend and I went to the cinema. We were young and full of life and instead of going straight home afterwards to obey the curfew we went to look at the shops to see all the latest fashions. So we were caught by the British soldiers and they were very angry. They beat us and made us take off our clothes. We were standing in the street wearing nothing, next to a clothes shop and my friend looked at the models in the window and said, "We are even worse off than those models, at least they have something to cover themselves."

'We both found this very funny and started to laugh and then we couldn't stop laughing but the soldiers became very angry and one of them attacked me with his rifle. He hit me in the face several times and knocked out my front teeth.'

At this point he paused in his storytelling to take out his false teeth and showed me the large gap where six or seven teeth had been smashed out. I also noticed for the first time that a long scar showed through the stubble of his left cheek.

'I cannot remember much after that but we had to spend some time locked up and I had to have my face fixed and then my life carried on as before, but I had scars on my face and inside me.

'A long time later I was walking on the beach with friends. You are a Varoshiotis so you remember our beautiful beach in Famagusta?' he digressed proudly.

'So I was walking on the beach and I saw the soldier who had hit me, sitting by the sea with his wife and children. A blinding anger welled up inside me and I lost control. I looked for a weapon, something to really hurt him with, anything with which to pay him back for what he did to me. There was nothing, the only thing I had was a chain around the waist of my swimming trunks. I took it off and ran over to him and beat him with it, I beat him badly. It was terrible, his wife and children were screaming and crying but I couldn't stop myself. My friends dragged me off him and took me away but I had to go to court. The judge took pity on me but he didn't need to punish me, I punished myself enough in the years that followed.'

I looked again at this quiet, gentle man. In his heart he had forgiven that soldier and forgiven the British and had sought me out to console me. He was the kind of man I was proud to call a friend. He stood up, tossed the stick aside and stretched his arms behind his back.

'So Kyrie Petro,' he said, carefully smoothing with his boots the marks he had made in the dust, 'You see we do crazy thing in the war. But we are man; all of us is just man.'

A game of tavli (backgammon) at the kafenion

The Kafenion

No Cypriot community can exist without a coffee shop and early on in our stay a small kiosk was brought to the camp and a crude open shelter built which, together with a few old chairs and benches, formed our kafenion. Sitting there I heard and overheard countless stories of loss and hardship, of lands lost and loved ones missing, of the treachery of power politics, of hopes for the future and dreams of a return home.

Those with 'missing' relatives suffered the most as they could not heal the open wound that the uncertainty caused. Those who knew their loved ones had died could gradually come to terms with their fate, but the lives of the relatives of the missing hung suspended in a world that fluctuated between hope and despair. At that time over 1,600 people were officially listed as missing; many had been seen as prisoners by others who had subsequently been released. In recent years graves have been exhumed and bodies identified using DNA techniques but to this day over 1,500 are still unaccounted for.[13]

But statistics never tell the whole story. To see the true impact on fragile lives you need to be close to those affected and this is what I experienced on the camp.

Images emerge sharply from the tangled undergrowth of my patchy memory. I see an ageing mother spending money she can ill afford to buy a large candle to burn in supplication to Saint Andrew after whom her missing son was named. I see two small girls framed in the viewfinder of my camera holding between them a photograph of their missing father. I see a bent old woman struggling to tighten the guy-ropes of her tent in a strong cold wind. I see a young woman, not knowing whether or not she is a widow, hunched over a concrete sink mechanically pounding clothes and staring blankly ahead at the corrugated iron wall of the communal washrooms. These ordinary people were paying a terrible price for a failure to avoid war.

The Turkish army was consolidating its grip on the north of the island and the trickle of new refugees into the camp became a stream. Time and again we heard stories of villagers coerced into agreeing to move to the south. They were usually given the choice to either sign a document to say they were leaving of their own free will and be given some days to pack the few things that they could carry, or not sign and face instant eviction with no opportunity to take even a few possessions.

---

[13] For further information see 'The Missing Cypriots Page' at www.missing-cy.org

Andreas's Kafenion-Taverna

The camp became busier and a second, unofficial, kafenion opened which, in addition to coffee, beer and nuts also served the most delicious souvlakia and sheftalia[14]. This raised it almost to the status of a taverna and I always thought of it as such. I always felt that Kyrios Andreas was not the most obvious person to run such a place. A man of few words, his long serious face seldom broke into a smile but he was friendly enough and enterprising and kept doggedly to his plan when rumours spread that his taverna had run into problems with the authorities.

The rumour that its construction, at the front of the camp close to the main road, had broken the law gave his shack a delicious clandestine air and the atmosphere within on a cold, dark night was magical. Everything about it was improvised: the roof, walls and doors (I do not remember any windows) were cobbled together from odds and ends found here and there. The rough wooden tables, benches and chairs were also gleaned oddments and well past their best. There was no electricity and the dim light cast by the paraffin lamps barely lit the stubbled faces of the men crowded together in the smoky air. These men were my idea of a real motley crew and their hand-me-down clothes showed a pragmatic disregard of taste or fashion and colourful combinations of colour and style were the order of the day. A dapper navy blue blazer, gratefully received from Western Europe, might be set off by a rough hessian sack across the shoulders or a glaring purple shirt complimented by layers of yellow, orange and green pullovers.

The atmosphere was almost always cheerful. Maybe it was the beer or the smell of the cooking food or just the feeling that they were as far down as they could get and yet could still enjoy the good things of life but, whatever it was, even when the wind shook the walls and rattled the door and the paraffin

---

[14] Souvlakia: charcoal grilled chunks of pork. Sheftalia: charcoal grilled minced meat and herb sausage.

lamps swung dangerously in the roof the men huddled inside continued to eat and drink and make merry.

On Thursday evenings it was always full beyond capacity and with good reason. The camp kitchens had a set weekly menu and some of the meals were delicious but on Thursday evenings, for reasons I still cannot understand, we were served sweet rice pudding topped with a slice of corned beef. On those nights the smell of souvlakia and the warm fug of the kafenion was a siren call that I was seldom able to resist.

Andreas was eventually compelled to dismantle this ramshackle building but, undeterred, he reconstructed it on the opposite side of the road and as business flourished enlarged and embellished it.

Fresh fruit and vegetables were brought to the camp by local growers

As soon as spring came and the weather grew dryer and warmer we were eager to leave our little room to embrace life under canvas and we selected two tents on the almost deserted western edge of the camp. May then used our room for children's classes. We had already been issued with camp beds and blankets, a folding table, a two ring gas cooker and other essentials and moved in easily using one tent as a living room and kitchen and the other as a bedroom. We found a small cupboard in a second hand shop that just fitted under the roof of the kitchen tent and were soon well settled and very comfortable.

Close to the front of our tents we had the shade of a small carob tree and sitting beneath it we enjoyed beautiful views down a slope of carob trees that fell gently to the west and the village of Kolossi beyond. In the cool of the evening we would watch the sun sink slowly into the distant horizon and listen to the muted sounds of camp life drifting to us on the evening breezes and counted ourselves lucky to be alive. This side of the camp was still without electricity and in the darkness after sunset the cicadas sang their shrill songs in the trees and the moon and stars hung huge and luminous in the sky.

The static walls and ceiling of a house can never match the magic of a tent on a moonlit night. Lying in bed we would watch the walls and roof heave and sink with the movement of the wind. The shadows on the white canvas would shift and change with every breath and the sound of the wind and creaking of the guy-ropes were a lullaby that soon lulled us to sleep.

In the early mornings a villager from Kolossi would drive his small heard of goats past our edge of the camp and we would often be woken by the soft, hollow ringing of their bells as they cropped the grass in front of our tents or tore leaves from the nearby carob trees. We felt safe and among friends and there was great tranquillity in having very little. There is no point in becoming fretful about possessions when all you have is in a tent with a toggled door that cannot be locked.

Goats heading homeward in the evening with our tents in the background

*

Tassos the fixer

A few newly arrived refugees gradually moved in around us but the serenity remained and one of them, Tassos who I named 'The Fixer', became a good friend. The Fixer was stocky and muscular and usually wore a sleeveless vest or went bare-chested. On Sundays and special occasions he had a taste for colourful Hawaiian shirts and this, together with his large unruly mop of black curly hair, swarthy complexion and full drooping moustache and sideburns, gave him a flamboyant devil-may-care demeanour.

Tassos was multi-talented and incredibly resourceful and procured all kinds of useful things from thin air. Impatient with waiting for the authorities to connect our electricity supply, he was soon to be seen up a telegraph pole with cable and pliers in hand and that evening we had electric light. I hardly dared mention to him that I needed anything as I was likely to find it lying outside our tents within a few days. He devised an excellent way of configuring the tents to give valuable extra shade by stretching horizontally and tying together the flysheets of adjoining tents. This created a shaded area between the two tents which unfortunately had a gap down the middle where the flysheets were too short to meet. Most people filled this gap with bamboo stems but the Fixer told me not to bother as he had a better solution. The next day I found a large sheet of green canvas just perfect for the job outside our door and gratefully fitted it in place. It was only some weeks later when I took a little used shortcut behind one of the unused marquees and saw a large rectangular hole about twice the size of my piece of canvas that I realized where it had come from.

Some people are impossible to keep down and if I were to learn that the Fixer is now a wealthy business man I would not be in the least surprised.

*

Life in the camp was never monotonous, something unusual was always happening, but some incidents were dramatic. My account of two such events that happened almost simultaneously follows.

Two dramas at Kolossi Camp

The sky was darkening. Low blue-grey clouds raced overhead and the wind moaned through the carob trees and around our tents sending the loose flaps snapping and cracking like pistol shots. A late winter's day was coming to a close and I was making my way to the centre of the camp where the communal kitchens stood.

In my hand I carried our family bowls. They were cheap, pink and plastic and into the bottom of each a Turkish name had been scratched. When they were issued to us Kyrios Stelios, the camp manager, explained that they had previously been used by Turkish prisoners of war, since released. We were the only refugees in the camp who could be expected to use them.

The strengthening wind pushed me along and almost whipped the bowls from my hand. A few heavy drops of rain thudded into the thick white canvas of the tents and rang on the corrugated iron of the newly built toilet block. I quickened my stride toward the lights of the kitchen, already quite bright in the gathering gloom.

The food for the refugees was prepared in this central kitchen and we collected it there and returned to our tents to eat. Small groups of women worked there on a rota basis under the supervision of two chefs employed by the government. Although the women were unpaid the work was taken very seriously and a 'No work, no food' policy was in force. The men had no such obligations. In fact every week two men were selected to do odd jobs around the camp for which they were paid.

As I drew closer to the kitchen I noticed a group of people standing in the pool of light from the open doorway and heard raised voices from within. This was unusual; something was going on. I edged my way through the small crowd in the doorway and into the cold glare of the fluorescent lighting where a dramatic little scene was being played out. Nearly everything in the kitchen was clean and well-scrubbed, the stainless steel and white enamel gleamed and the starched white outfits of the chefs stood out in contrast to the ragamuffin clothes of the refugees. Used clothing from overseas had arrived in sacks at the camp and was gratefully received as many had fled their homes in only light summer clothing. The ragged line that formed a rough queue for food and the onlookers who had already filled their bowls were a patchwork of incongruous colours and styles, vivid against the whitewashed concrete of the kitchen walls.

In the centre of the room and at the head of the queue, still and implacable, stood a tall finely built woman with light hair and a bronzed weathered face. At her side stood her son, swarthy and black haired, a heavy stubble on his young face. I knew most of the refugees and their backgrounds and was aware that the father of this family was missing, probably dead, and that this boy was now the oldest male of a family of five. It was his voice I had heard from outside and, in contrast to his mother's stillness, he gesticulated wildly giving emphasis to his words with forceful gestures.

His adversary was the head chef; an elderly man, small and stooping with neat grey hair and gold rimmed spectacles. He looked unusually frail that evening but he was sure of himself and stood his ground without flinching. It seemed that the woman had not done her work in the kitchen and the 'No work, no food' rule was being enforced. She may have had a good reason for missing her rotas as whenever her son made a point and paused there were murmurs of agreement from among the refugees.

The chef too had his supporters and his quietly spoken words were met with nods and short speeches of support. As the argument intensified fewer people joined in until only the young man and the chef remained; the one shouting furiously, scarcely pausing for breath the other becoming very still, his voice hardening to a cold whisper. Suddenly something inside the youngster snapped. He pushed the old man away from the food and it looked like a fight was about to start when there was a great scream from outside and an old woman burst through the doorway and pushed past me into the room.

'Fire!' She shrieked, gasping for breath, her wrinkled face alive with fear. 'Fire, the tents are on fire!'

What I have always loved about the Cypriots is their instinctive sense of drama. They display their emotions in the most theatrical way absolutely naturally. The old woman who burst into the kitchen turned from side to side to take in her whole audience as she gasped out her news like a messenger of doom in a Greek tragedy.

The kitchen emptied quickly and I never knew how that drama ended for I was now caught up in another, rushing up the hill in the half dark towards the blazing tents. Some might say the cojaggary[15] had exaggerated a little, only two tents were on fire but the sight of them alarmed us all. The wind was now almost a gale, howling in the guy ropes and overhead wires, tugging at loose clothing and canvas. Everyone was yelling, it was the only way to be heard, ordinary speech was whipped away on the wind. But above the sound of the wind and the shouting rose the frightening sound of the fire. The flames were devouring everything with a dreadful roaring, savagely tearing the heart out of those makeshift homes. The tent that had caught first was already collapsing in on itself. Incandescent skeletons of objects stood for a few moments in the leaping flames, glowing white in the shuddering wind, then dropped inwards noiselessly sending huge clouds of sparks high into the air and down the scorched path of the wind.

It was to the tents downwind that our attention turned. Two tents were lost and a third had started to burn. Hungry little fingers of flame were already running along the edges of the awning sheet. Shouts had gone up for bowls and buckets and now water was being brought in any container available to quench the flames. We, who a few moments earlier had stood rooted in the kitchen, now rushed frantically back and forth from the fire to the sinks and back again and again. Water was

---

[15] Cojaggary An elderly woman, usually a widow, always dressed in black

flung onto the fires and the scorched white canvas of the third tent. Our containers were pitifully small and stumbling over the uneven ground in the half-light we spilt plenty but after what seemed an age we could see that we had won. We had saved the other tents.

The fire had lost some of its force now and had settled down to a relentless gnawing of the more solid things at its heart. Suddenly a voice bellowed from the darkness

'The gas! The gas will explode!'

The couple whose tents had burned had just arrived back in the camp and the man had seen a danger all of us had missed. He came out of the darkness and into the glare of the flames running. I don't know whether he was driven by fear or anger or despair but he came straight on and without pausing for a moment plunged into the blazing ruins. Rotten with fire they crumbled around him and he gave the large gas bottle a kick that sent it spinning to safety. Great clouds of sparks rose high into the air but in another stride he was out the other side, a little burned and dazed but unhurt. Friends dragged him away and brushed embers from his clothing but he had eyes only for the fire.

I shall never forget the look in that man's eyes. It was not anger or fear or frustration; it was resignation, a bitter resignation that simply could not understand. "Whatever I have done in my life", it seemed to say "I have not deserved this."

Imagine, if you can, what it is to lose almost everything you have, to carry a few precious things to a safer place and to try to start again. Then even those things are taken from you and you have nothing. All this was written on his face more clearly than I can write it here. His wife had been standing close to me supported by a little crowd of friends. She had seemed mesmerised but now she gave a piercing shriek and threw herself onto the stony ground.

'My photographs.' She sobbed, 'My wedding, my mother.' Nothing could ever bring these things back and the thought seemed to drive her into a hysterical frenzy. She kicked and screamed, clawing at the hard earth with her bare hands. Red polished nails broke on stone and I turned away, it was all too much.[16]

Red and sullen now with only a few licking flames the fire had almost burned itself out and I made my way back to the kitchen and collected our food. The place was almost deserted leaving only the chefs speculating quietly over a glass of beer about the cause of the fire. I went out once more into the wind and darkness looking with new eyes at our bowls of beans. Our pink plastic bowls with names scratched on them by unknown Turks, themselves refugees. And I thought about war.

Visitors

Expletive Forgiven 1

Most of the government workers who ran the camp were themselves refugees who were unable to return to their normal professions. Their salaries had been severely reduced but they could still afford to live off the camp and preferred to do so. Most were teachers but there were also social workers and health visitors and at times the small office would become quite crowded. I was usually called there when important visitors such as politicians, foreign diplomats or journalists arrived. There was no lack of English speakers but I think I was a novelty and my solidarity with the refugees was considered good publicity.

A few of the refugee men spoke a particular version of English which I termed 'Squaddie'. They had worked alongside British soldiers for many years and gradually picked up their language which, unfortunately, included the frequent use of expletives. Innocent of what they were saying when speaking English these refugees literally swore like troopers.

---

[16] The Limassol Fire Brigade arrived later and made the area safe. Days later they returned with a considerable sum of money they had collected for the family whose tents had been burned

On one occasion when we were entertaining the Commercial Attaché of an eastern European state two men were drafted in to prepare tea. Some of us had already been served when the very formal conversation was interrupted by one of them who, standing in the middle of the crowded office, politely cleared his throat and said,

'Please excuse for the delay everyone but we no have enough f***ing cups.'

As I tried to choke back my laughter a mouthful of tea forced its way up my nose and tears started to stream from my eyes. I coughed to hide my embarrassment and smiled benignly to the gathered diplomats whose English was fortunately not good enough to understand this undiplomatic language.

Expletive Forgiven 2

Very welcome visitors to the camp were those who came to entertain. These were usually choirs of school children but we were once given an excellent traditional "Karagiozis" shadow puppet show. Like Mr Punch in western European Punch and Judy shows, Karagiozis is a loveable rogue who is always trying to outwit authority figures in order to gain food or money and his story has a folk tradition as long and varied as Punch himself.

The visit I remember most vividly was a group of young children who came in the days leading up to Christmas and sang carols for us. It was a cold, bright day and the strong wind that swept across the camp tugged at guy ropes and sent light bits and pieces flying. The refugees were all gathered in one of the large marquees and when I arrived it was standing room only so I slipped in at the back, glad to escape from the wind that seemed intent on ripping every tent from the ground. It was only a little warmer in the shelter of the marquee and I was glad to see that everyone was warmly clothed. Before the singing could start two men were dispatched to tighten the guy ropes and secure the cracking flaps that threatened to drown out the voices of the children. They returned to stand next to me and the choir began to sing.

No singing that I have ever heard before or since has ever affected me so profoundly. I did not understand the words being sung but the sound was divine. Sweet young voices rose above the sound of the wind and everything seemed to be part of a harmonious whole: the swelling voices of the choir, the heaving canvas walls and ceiling and the moaning wind all came together to create a beauty beyond mere music. The contrast between the ravaged lives of this ragged group of refugees and the naive young faces that looked back at them was heart rending and I had to bite my lip as a few people began to cry.

To finish, they sang 'Silent Night', first in Greek then in English. The broad, sack covered, shoulders of a large man at the front began to shake as more people broke down in tears. Those of us determined not to cry could not prevent tears spilling down our cheeks. It seemed that the whole marquee was sobbing but the singing children carried on to the end. I have heard many renditions of that carol since but nothing can match the sincerity of those flawless young voices. The sound was like pure clear water compared to which the renditions offered up during the Christmas period today in shopping malls and supermarkets are like old, flat Coca-Cola.

As we pushed our way out of the marquee I was in another world, my head full of the sounds of the soughing wind, the sobbing and the pure sweet singing. I was brought sharply back to earth when one of the men who had secured the ropes turned to me and, wiping tears from his stubbled face, bitterly muttered 'F***ing Americans.'[17]

---

[17] Many refugees felt that the Americans had engineered the Coup d'état and the subsequent Turkish invasion.

The media

Time passed and the word must have been spread among foreign journalists that there was an Englishman living on the Kolossi camp because we started to get a steady trickle of them. Many of them were hard-bitten professionals who had spent a lifetime covering disaster areas around the world and in general they made light of the plight of the refugees. Being highly mobile themselves they couldn't see the swapping of a house in the north for a house in the south as much of a problem. I tried to explain how deeply rooted the village people were to their ancestral homes but felt that my words fell on ears deafened by years spent hearing of too much tragedy.

There were two notable exceptions to this cynical attitude. One was a BBC radio journalist, whose name I cannot remember but who I will call Jonathan, who arrived with his producer late one afternoon in early autumn. We all sat drinking tea on a low bench in front of our tents and had a long and relaxed conversation along the usual lines of how we came to be on the camp and what we were doing to help people there.

It was then decided that we were ready to start recording so sound checks were made and Jonathan began his introduction with a few matters of fact concerning date, place and interviewee that were clearly not designed for broadcast. He then paused, took a deep breath and underwent a complete change of personality. Gone was the man I'd chatted with for the last hour and in his place was a master wordsmith, declaiming like a Shakespearian actor.

'To the west soft blue-green skies fade to rose toward the setting sun.' he began 'Above me wispy white clouds form, melt and reform in an azure sky and behind me a thousand gleaming white tents march, rank upon rank, to the horizon. This is Kolossi refugee camp and I am sitting in front of the tent of an English refugee, Peter Moore who lives here with his family.' He paused, then,

'Peter, why?'

I was completely tongue-tied, still up in the azure sky with the wispy clouds. After what seemed a very long time I managed to stammer,

'Err... can we start again please?'

And we did. Unperturbed, Jonathan, the consummate professional, did exactly the same introduction but this time I was ready and everything went well.

The other exception was Nick McCarty, an author and playwright who found me one day sitting under a carob tree to the north of the camp flying a kite. On enquiring after me at the camp office the kite was pointed out and he was told I would be on the other end of the string. He enjoyed this introduction and we became friends immediately and remain so to this day. He did not share my love of kites but he had long been in love with Cyprus and we shared a desire to help if we could. Nick wrote extensively about the war and its aftermath and had an in-depth knowledge of the political scene that I lacked at the time. He had a son about the same age as Zim and our families met up several times that summer and over the following years.

Melina Mercouri

Melina Mercouri was a famous Greek film star and singer and the extraordinary thing about her visit to the camp is that I have no recollection of it whatsoever so have to rely on a recent interview with K. Stelios Panayides and film posted on the internet. I am told there was great excitement on the camp and a large crowd gathered to welcome her. She arrived with a large entourage which included a film crew to record her latest song 'Cypriot Woman' which was to be included in a documentary she was making about the plight of the Cypriots.

Flowers were presented and welcoming speeches were made and an emotional performance followed with Melina moving among the gathered refugees as she sang. The performance was repeated time and again until the director was satisfied. The film shows children being caressed and black clad crying women consoled and I have no doubt my fellow refugees felt comforted.

I do not understand why I have forgotten all this but suspect that it was all too sentimental for me and I have blocked it from my memory.

Women walk home

In the spring a group of three women representing the island-wide organisation Women Walk Home visited the camp in search of an Irish woman refugee married to a Cypriot who they had heard lived there. Women Walk Home, a group of women of various nationalities living in Cyprus, were organising a peaceful march to publicise the fact that women could not walk home because the island was militarily divided and were looking for volunteers to march with them carrying the flags of their countries.

The three visitors were an appropriate mix of nationalities themselves being from Denmark, England and Holland. They were delighted to find that there was another non-Cypriot woman on the camp and came to see May. May has British nationality but her parents were Persian and she was born in Bahrain and, after some discussion to ascertain that no politics were involved, she agreed to carry the flag of Bahrain.

We discovered that the Dutch lady, Marion Pnevmaticos, had a son, Philip, almost exactly the same age as Zim and she arranged to come back with her family. We became the best of friends with her and her husband, Takis, and remain so to this day.

The walk back to homes in Famagusta was stopped at the Green Line, as expected, but the sight of thirty thousand silent women, led by those carrying the fluttering flags of many nationalities was a stirring site and, in terms of the publicity generated, achieved its aim.

Family

To our great delight news came that my twin brother, Paul, with his partner Lynnie, were to pay us a visit on their way to Kathmandu. I went to the port in Limassol and watched as their boat gradually grew from a speck in the distance to a large ferry tying up at the dockside and above my head and I could see them waving excitedly. Until I had hugged them both for a few minutes I could not believe they were really there but soon we were heading through the citrus orchards of Phassouri to the camp. Unfortunately, in my excitement I had forgotten to put petrol in the car and it sputtered to a halt among the tall cypresses that protected the orchards. The first task for our visitors, who found the whole business hilarious, was to collect fuel for me and to this day they refer to that place as 'No petrol bend'.

They had seen pictures on British television of the hastily constructed ramshackle camps thrown up in the immediate aftermath of the war and were expecting to find us living in rather squalid conditions but were pleasantly surprised to see our well-kept camp with its gleaming white tents and excellent facilities. Having camped across Europe they rated the toilet and shower units as among the best they had seen on their trip. They were made welcome by the camp officials and were offered a tent and food from the kitchens which they politely declined but gratefully accepted the use of the washing and toilet facilities. We did notice, however, that after their arrival our rations seemed to increase.

After a little reconnoitring our visitors set up their tent under the shelter of carob trees at the bottom of the western slope below our tents. Memorable days and evenings followed as we caught up with each other's news, discussed the political situation, swam, visited archaeological sites, played cards and laughed a lot.

They were impressed by the efforts of the camp managers to create a feeling of community by organising well attended social events. These usually took the form of musical performances by visiting professionals who gave their time freely and were warmly received. The determination of the people to bounce back from adversity also impressed them. The fortitude of a near neighbour who quietly picked her freshly washed clothes out of the dust when her washing line broke and went uncomplaining to the washing huts to do it all again was just one example and they gradually became accustomed to seeing people with very little making great efforts to improve their lot. Lynnie was amazed one morning to find that the newlyweds who were our next door neighbours were holding a Tupperware party in their tent. This was not as incongruous as it seemed as the tents of many refugees were at some distance from the kitchen and food carried in open bowls got cold. A simple lidded container was the perfect solution.

Paul was dismayed that the beautiful island on which he found himself was riven by inter-communal strife and political shenanigans. His outspoken comments, which could at heated moments develop into ranting, sometimes caused trouble. On one occasion a meeting at St. Johns School in the Episkopi Sovereign Base Area was brought to a swift halt when he demanded to know why the British were in Cyprus at all if they were not prepared to do their duty as a guarantor power to protect its independence.

A more dangerous outburst occurred when he tried to visit the Turkish held area. Tensions were still high on the 'Green Line' dividing the two communities but we passed through the Cypriot and UN manned posts at the Ledra Palace crossing in Nicosia without difficulty. By this time Paul had become accustomed to being stopped by 'Boys with machine guns and dirty boots', to use his own phrase, but he was not prepared for the high handed attitude of the Turkish military. A table had been set up on the dusty ground in front of a portable office at which sat a smartly dressed officer flanked by two armed soldiers. The incongruity of the officer seated at his desk was emphasised by a number of stray chickens that pecked busily around him, scratching in the dry earth in search of food. He examined Paul and Lynnie's passports thoroughly and in perfect English said,

'We cannot allow you to pass as you have entered the country illegally'.

'But,' my brother protested, 'We came into Limassol port.'

'That is a Greek held port,' replied the officer, 'and it is illegal.'

At this point Paul became dangerously irate.

'You people are all idiots.' he fumed. 'You have this beautiful little island and all you do is fight about what is Turkish and what is Greek'.

Beginning to rant he gesticulated wildly to a nearby chicken.

'Look at that chicken.' he shouted. 'Do you think the chicken would say "Oh, before the war I was a Greek chicken but now I'm a Turkish chicken." No, the chicken would say. "I live in Cyprus, I'm a Cyprus chicken." You are an idiot. The chickens here have more brains than you.'

By this time the soldiers, who could clearly not understand a word of what was being said but saw a long haired foreigner shouting at their officer, were becoming agitated and they started to shuffle towards the table fingering their triggers. I quickly pulled Paul away before things got out of hand and we hurriedly left the officer, his soldiers and his chickens without giving him the right to reply. I had learned to bite my tongue but Paul fumed for the next few days and still gets excited when recalling the incident.

Paul and Lynnie loved Cyprus so much they decided to stay for a while and rented a small, almost derelict, old house in Kolossi village where they lived until late autumn. They had run out of time to go to Kathmandu long ago and so headed back to England leaving behind an empty space in our lives that never quite filled.

During their stay I had been able to get into Famagusta and it was their car, which crucially had a roof-rack, that I borrowed for the trip.

Paul and Lynnie arrive at the camp

Glimpses of Famagusta

It was late spring 1975 and the Turkish authorities had let it be known that expatriate refugees could apply to return to Famagusta to retrieve their possessions. I had mixed feelings about this decision as it seemed to indicate that the many rumours that all refugees were soon to be allowed back to their homes in the city were untrue but early one morning I journeyed to Nicosia to try my luck. The taxi dropped me at the Ledra Palace crossing and I explained my mission to the soldiers on the Greek Cypriot side. They wished me luck and I left the safety of their checkpoint and headed out across the no-man's-land they called the Green Line toward the Turkish checkpoint. To my left a United Nations flag flew above the scarred façade of the Ledra Palace hotel reminding me that the two sides often exchanged fire across this space at night and I walked as fast as I could without giving the watching soldiers the idea that I was anxious. It was a lonely walk, these were the early days of the border being opened to a few expatriates and no-one else was taking the chance that morning.

I approached the Turkish barrier with some trepidation. I had watched the Turkish army training in the old walled city of Famagusta and knew that they were pretty hard men but the formality of passport checking went smoothly and I was directed to a nearby office where Turkish Cypriot bureaucrats waited.

This was to be the first of many visits that I made to the Turkish side to try to get permission to return to our home and take our belongings. That morning I was treated with polite respect and thereafter the Turkish Cypriot authorities were always courteous but it was a convoluted process and progress was very slow. Just when I thought I had fulfilled all the requirements new demands would be made. On one occasion I went, as requested, with an inventory of the contents of our house, listed room by room. This had not been easy as we had been away for almost a year and, as I handed it over, I hoped I had overcome the last hurdle. The official looked carefully through the long and detailed list and eventually looked up with a kindly smile.

'Mr Moore, I need to see receipts for all the items you have listed here'.

For months I had been making the long journey from the refugee camp in the south of the island to Nicosia and my patience had worn thin.

'Even if I had kept receipts do you think that when I had to leave my house I would take them with me rather than the things themselves?'

He looked perplexed but stuck to the official line.

'You must bring me the receipts for all these items or I cannot allow you to go back to your house'

'The shirt you're wearing.' I said. 'Do you have the receipt for it?'

I was aware that my voice was rising but I was past caring and began to rant.

'Nobody keeps receipts that long. Most of those things I brought with me from England anyway. This is completely ridiculous!'

Polite and implacable he told me that I would have to produce the receipts or forget about retrieving our belongings and I left the office angry and frustrated. I realised later that the Turkish Cypriot authorities were powerless to allow anyone back into Famagusta without the permission of the Turkish military and that these impossible demands were stalling tactics to allow the army to go about their business unseen by the outside world.

The receipts requirement was eventually dropped and sometime later I was given permission to join a convoy into the deserted city with a view to retrieving documents that would prove beyond doubt that my family had lived in our house at the time of the war.

It was in July 1975, almost exactly a year after leaving, that I joined a convoy from Nicosia and drove my brother's beetle into the abandoned city. It was eerily quiet, a ghost town baking in the summer heat. Tall weeds grew through the tarmac of what had been busy shopping streets downtown and in the residential areas clothes hung listlessly on washing lines in silent testament to hurried departures. A sense of desolation and tragic waste hung in the hot fetid air.

We had suspected that our house had been looted as we had been able to see our veranda at the back of the house through binoculars from the village of Dherinia[18] and had seen that one of the French windows was open. Despite this forewarning the chaotic scene that greeted me when I opened our front door was a great shock.

---

[18]Dherinia is located on a hill just south of Famagusta and today has a small museum and a lookout post with binoculars from where visitors can view the desolate city.

Everything had been pulled down from the extensive bookshelves and thrown from the desks and chests and lay scattered in heaps on the floor. It was difficult to walk without stepping on something precious and I asked Mehmet, my allocated Turkish Cypriot official, to ask the two soldiers who accompanied us to be careful where they trod.

Mehmet left after a few minutes leaving me to look for the required documents under the watchful eyes of the soldiers and I started to search through the piles of books, letters and papers to find them. It was as though wild animals had rampaged through our home oblivious of the sentimental bonds attached to so much of what they flung about at random. Anyone whose home has been burgled and trashed knows the feeling of violation that it brings; the mixture of anger and distress, of outrage and sorrow. I tried to compose myself and worked as fast as I could, trying hard to focus on the task at hand, but when I saw one of the soldiers standing on the beautiful white sari that May had worn as her wedding dress something snapped.

I yelled at him but he didn't understand and simply stared at me impassively whilst tightening his grip on his rifle. The poor boy represented the whole sickening repressive system[19] to me in that moment and I wanted to attack him with my bare hands but, fortunately, discretion became the better part of valour. Fighting but failing to keep my emotions in check, I pushed him gently to one side and carefully removed the now dirty sari from under his dusty boots.

In the short time before Mehmet returned I had not been able to find all the specified documents I needed but he assured me that what I had, together with a few others not on the list, would be ample evidence that the house was mine. I quickly looked over the rest of the house, checking on precious things that I had hidden before leaving. They were all still there but so were the watching soldiers who followed me everywhere

---

[19] The Turkish Cypriots at the time would have seen the Turkish army as their saviours and protectors. It is unclear how many would still see it that way nearly forty years later.

and I realised later that to reveal these hiding places was a mistake.

With a mixture of sadness and relief I left the house and followed Mehmet down to the seafront where an English restaurant owner was loading his things onto a dilapidated lorry. I offered to help but he explained that the one lorry he had been allocated was already overloaded and he would have to leave the rest behind. I suggested that I could carry a few chairs and curtains in my car and he readily agreed.

When I started to load the chairs onto the roof-rack I heard an angry shout from behind but I didn't understand Turkish and, tired of being dictated to by rifle carrying boys, I carried on regardless. I was just loading the second chair when I heard Mehmet's voice ring out in alarm first in Turkish and then in English.

"Mr Moore do not move! Do not move!"
I froze while an animated conversation took place behind me and when I did eventually look over my shoulder I saw a Turkish soldier slowly lowering his gun.

I'm not sure how close I came to getting shot that day but Mehmet explained to me that the soldiers were under orders to shoot anyone they caught looting and that is what I appeared to be doing. When we were safely back in the government controlled area the restaurateur insisted I keep everything I had brought out and in the fullness of time the chairs and curtains graced our new home for many years.

I left the documents I had collected with the authorities and was told to return in a week or so when I expected to be given a date to return to Famagusta to collect our belongings. I should have known better.

'Mr Moore, we asked you to collect certain documents but you have not done so. I am afraid you cannot go to Famagusta again.'

'But Mehmet said that what I collected was adequate proof that the house was my residence.'

'Mehmet? Who is Mehmet? He has no authority to change the requirements. Maybe I can arrange for you to go in again. I don't know, I can't promise. Maybe. Come back next week.'

Once again I left the office angry and frustrated vowing to have nothing more to do with such frustrating and irrational people. However, the prospect of retrieving our precious things was too strong a motivator to be denied for long (Zim was particularly anxious to get his little bicycle back!) and I eventually calmed down enough to ring the authorities a few days later. To my surprise and delight I was given a date to go in with a lorry to get our things. No explanation was ever given for the change of heart and I didn't ask any probing questions fearing another reversal.

Excited and pleased I arranged for one of the lorry drivers who delivered supplies to the camp to meet us at the Ledra Palace on the Green Line on the allotted day. The lorry that would carry our things from Famagusta was allocated to us by the Turkish Cypriot authorities but it could only return as far as the Ledra Palace border crossing so a Greek Cypriot lorry was needed onto which our things could be transferred for the journey south.

The allocation of lorries was a bit like Russian roulette. Expatriates could be allocated any number of drivers and driver's mates; the most I heard of was eight to clear the small bungalow of a close friend. This not only cost him a large sum of money for the hiring fee but looting was rife and it was impossible to keep an eye on so many people.

Luckily we were allocated just one lorry and May and I followed it into Famagusta where not much had changed since my last visit except that most of the shops had now been emptied. We eventually arrived at our house in the unavoidable company of two armed soldiers and I opened the front door with some anxiety but everything seemed as it was the last time I was there. May is a strong character and I had prepared her for what to expect but the sight of our ravaged home was hard to take. It took a few minutes but soon I saw a familiar determined look on her face and a fierce glint in her eyes and we got down to work. Once again we had limited time and we rushed to pack everything as best we could. I still find it painful to recall the details of our scramble to get our things packed and onto the lorry in the heat, in a short space of time and under the eyes of two bored but watchful armed soldiers. The driver and his mate were helpful at first but would mysteriously disappear occasionally and we had no time or energy to chase after them. By now I had learned to live with impotent rage but when the driver returned after one foray with his arms full of carpets from our neighbours' houses I struggled to contain my anger. I was paying for this man to help me and he was stealing from my friends and I could do nothing to stop him.

The precious things I had made sure were safe on my first visit were gone from their hiding places, among them a set of original BBC transcription recordings of 'The Goon Show'. I was very sorry to lose them but it amused me later to think of a mystified Turk somewhere listening to those records and desperately trying to make sense of what he heard.

Eventually the job was done and although in the rush we had to leave some of our belongings behind we had been able to recover most of the important things. Unfortunately they did not include Zim's little bicycle. As we drove away from our house I thought of my neighbours. Compared to them we were the lucky ones. They would never get back to their homes and would never retrieve the precious things they had left behind.

We were driven to the military headquarters in the city where we were obliged to sign a statement saying that we had found our house and its contents intact and had removed all our possessions and for this we thanked the Turkish authorities. This was a difficult pill to swallow but our belongings would not be allowed out of the city until it was done so I composed a carefully worded statement in which I said that I had taken all of my possessions that I had found in my house. The nuanced meaning went undetected and we were soon trundling across the Mesaoria[20] toward Nicosia keeping a watchful eye on our things in the lorry ahead.

---

[20]The Mesaoria is a broad, fertile plain which makes up the

We had heard that if the convoy slowed or stopped at certain points it was so that booty could be thrown to waiting accomplices by the roadside. I cannot say whether or not this was true but there were things that we remembered loading in Famagusta that we could not find when we reached the Green line.

Socrates, the camp lorry driver, was waiting for us in no-man's land but his mate was nowhere to be seen.

'Where is Bambos?' we asked. Socrates looked slightly embarrassed.

'Bambos, he is little bit fearful. He is stay on the Greek side. Like to have a drink in the bar with UN soldiers'

'But is he coming to help?'

'I think so no. He is too much afraid'

A polite exchange took place between the two drivers and we got on with the work. In order that Socrates (and through him the entire Greek Cypriot race) would not lose face we made excuses for Bambos' absence. It was, after all, no small thing to come so close to armed Turkish soldiers who had a fearful reputation.

We had transferred about half of our things onto Socrates lorry when the sound of distant singing caused us to look in the direction of the Greek Cypriot lines. Bambos was making his uncertain way towards us and was keeping his spirits up with a jaunty Greek song. He had obviously had enough of another kind of spirit to find the courage to venture toward the Turkish lines. Unsure just how popular the loud singing of a Greek song would be with the Turkish soldiers we called to Bambos to be quiet and to come to the lorry. He completely ignored us and with unsteady steps made his way to the nearest soldier who was standing to attention at his post. Bambos stopped uncomfortably close to him and, swaying slightly from side to side, fumbled in the top pocket of his shirt for his cigarettes.

'Here my friend,' he said in Greek, 'Do you smoke?

---

centre of the island.

The soldier stood implacable staring at close range into Bambos' eyes. Undeterred, Bambos pushed the cigarette packet up under the soldier's nose.

'Do you smoke my friend? Eh? Eh? Ah, OK, you don't smoke. Good, good, is better. Is better not to smoke.' He put a cigarette between his own lips and continued.

'Me, I like too much to smoke the cigarette.'

The unlit cigarette flicked up and down dangerously close to the soldier's face.

Bambos fumbled in his trousers for his matches and after a few attempts lit it. He inhaled deeply and, standing open mouthed on the back of the lorry, I willed him not to blow the smoke into the Turk's face but he turned at the last moment and the cloud of smoke drifted harmlessly into the air. He stood beside the soldier for a time philosophising on the evils of smoking and ignoring our calls but eventually we were relieved to see him turn and stumble towards us. The broad smile on his face showed how pleased he was with himself and he greeted Socrates like a long lost friend. Bambos didn't do much work that day but kept us and the Cypriots of both communities entertained with light hearted banter and snatches of songs.

Before long we were again following a lorry loaded with our things but this time we were heading south where we would put them into storage until we left the camp. It had been a long and difficult day but all had ended happily. We had safely retrieved most of our things, we had survived the emotional turmoil of seeing and then leaving again our home in Famagusta and Bambos, who was slowly sobering up in the lorry ahead, had not been shot but had given us an unforgettable memory. He had reminded me again of why I had such affection for the people of Cyprus.

Photography

Early on in our days on the camp I bought a cheap Russian Lubitel II twin lens reflex camera that, despite its price, produced sharp, well defined pictures. I wanted to record life on the camp and took a reel of twelve photographs which I posted up on the door of the communal kitchen. A small crowd soon gathered and, although I could not understand most of their remarks, it was clear that I had made a welcome addition to camp life. Those featured in the photos asked for copies and some asked if I could go to their tents and take family photos. Most wanted multiple copies so that they could send reassuring pictures to their relatives oversees.

I had made friends with a kind Englishman, Pat Thompson, who owned a camera shop in Polemidhia and he generously printed the photos for me at cost price. He charged me nothing for his time and I hoped later that, as demand grew way beyond what either of us expected, he didn't mind working for nothing. Demand soon grew to the point where I had to limit my photography sessions to Sunday mornings when I would go to everyone who had booked a session in my hastily devised diary during the preceding week.

Zim and his good friends Alexia and Philip Pnevmaticos

*Proud and defiant, this picture seems to say
'Our homes have been taken but not our dignity'*

Sometimes the sessions would be straightforward; the family would be in their best clothes and would arrange themselves into a formal group and stand ready to be photographed. They always wanted to look reassuringly happy and I seldom managed to get an informal, unposed shot. Photographing the younger people, especially the young men, was far more time consuming.

Stavros was typical of the young men. Dressed fashionably in the flared trousers and large collared shirts of the mid-seventies, his unruly long hair temporarily tamed by a quick sprinkling of water he would want to place himself in exactly the right location in exactly the right position. With his bronzed face turned toward my lenses wearing his "I am a man to be taken seriously" expression he would need to know if his watch was showing below the cuff of his shirt and if the buckle of his belt was clearly visible and the details of every other combination of position, clothing and adornment possible. On one occasion the fingers of one hand which had been placed on his hip were carefully moved to exactly the right place by the free hand. By the time all of this was set up perfectly his cigarette would have burned down to an unacceptable level and a fresh one would be lit and we would start all over again.

With one person this was time consuming but with a group of three or four friends it became a saga as these elements would be multiplied by the number of people involved. The added issue of who was standing next to who and how the poses reflected their various relationships now came into play and there were times when I feared the session would go on for ever.

All the young dudes

One of my favourite subjects was an older man called Lalakis who I named Zorba as he seemed to embody the larger than life, defiant anarchy of Nikos Kazantzakis's character. Lalakis was a fine figure of a man, tall and barrel-chested with a full head of wavy greying hair and a fine moustache. No matter in what situation I photographed him he always struck a heroic pose, his chest out, his head held high, his eyes gazing meaningfully into the middle distance. In one picture he raises a hand in greeting to the world at large. He was very hard working and resourceful and spoke good English and he helped me enormously when working on projects.

The indomitable Lalakis

His wife was Irish ("I rescued her from a nunnery Petros. She was to have been a nun but when she saw me ...", a pause and then a roar of laughter), but she had lived the Cypriot village life for so long she seemed reluctant to speak her native tongue.

Near the end of our stay in the camp and after I had stopped working for the refugee authorities, Zorba found work for a small team of refugees digging on a Bronze Age archaeological excavation nearby and I felt honoured to be invited to join them. It was fascinating work but unbearably hot working in shallow pits with tiny trowels painstakingly scraping the earth under a blazing summer sun.

I never tired of the photography sessions, they were a source of pleasure for me and I was happy to do something that brightened the lives of my fellow refugees a little. The surviving photographs are a testament to their indomitable spirit. In the posed pictures they stand proud and tall and look the world in the eye. Later pictures show the areas around their tents are clean and tidy and in some cases small gardens have been created. One shows a group from the same village next to a sign they have erected showing their village name (ΒΑΤΥΛΗ = VATILI).

Looking at those pictures now is to run the full gambit of emotions. Some show mothers or wives or children holding photographs of their missing relatives. In others bewildered elderly couples sit outside their tents trying to look stoical and composed. Happier photos show groups from the youth club, the football team or the icon makers. The most heartening show children smiling and laughing as they pose happily in their bleak surroundings.

A small selection from the hundreds of pictures I took fill the following pages.

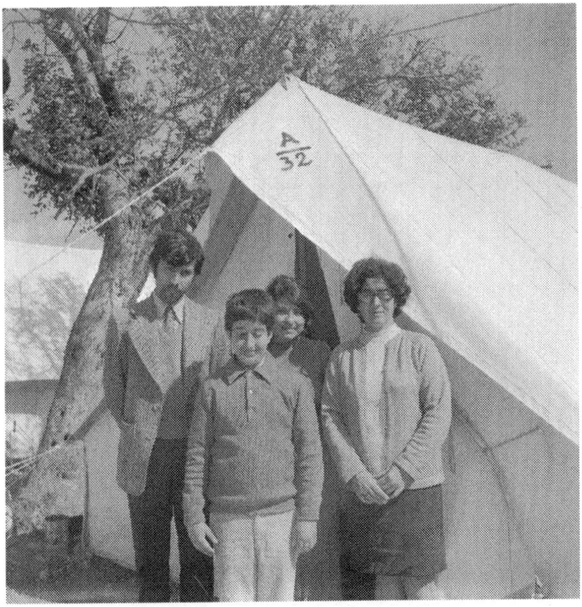
A
32

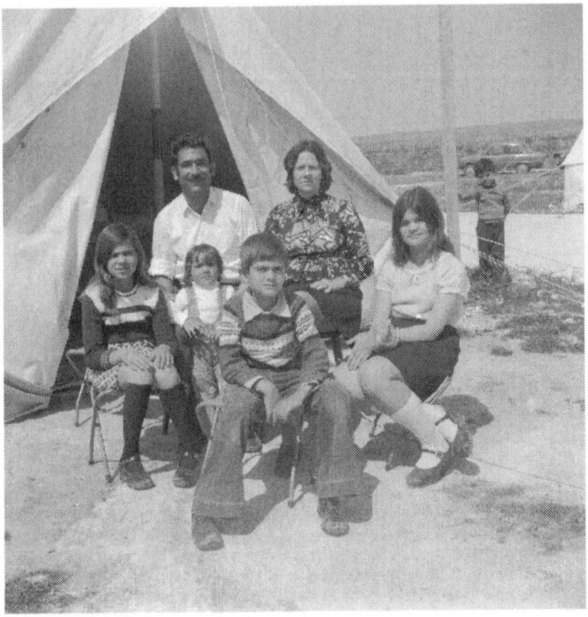

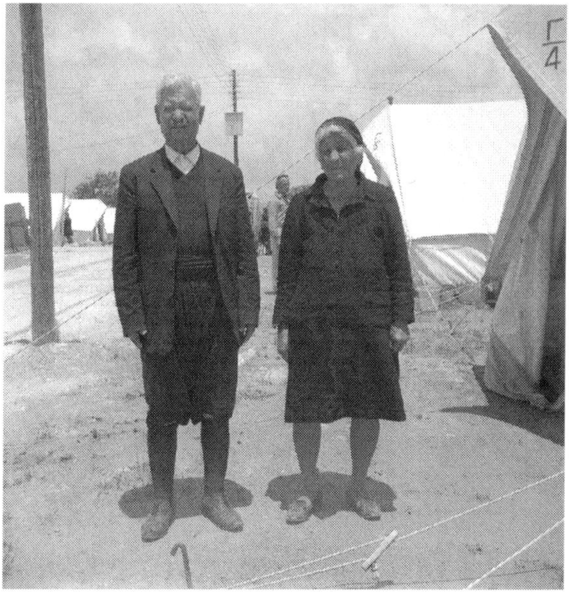
Γ
4

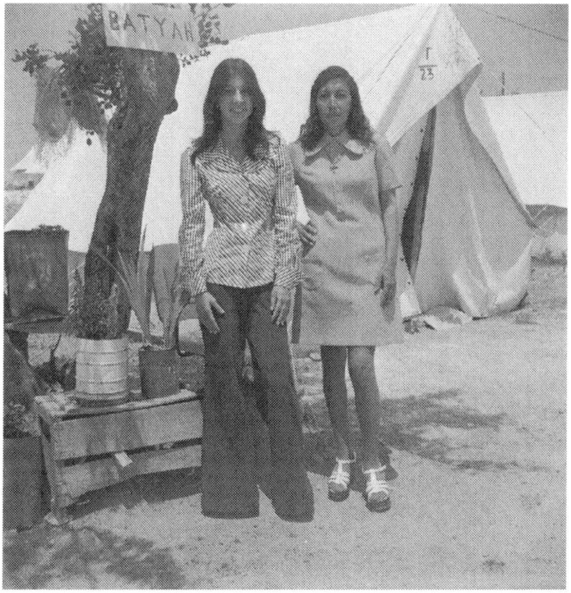

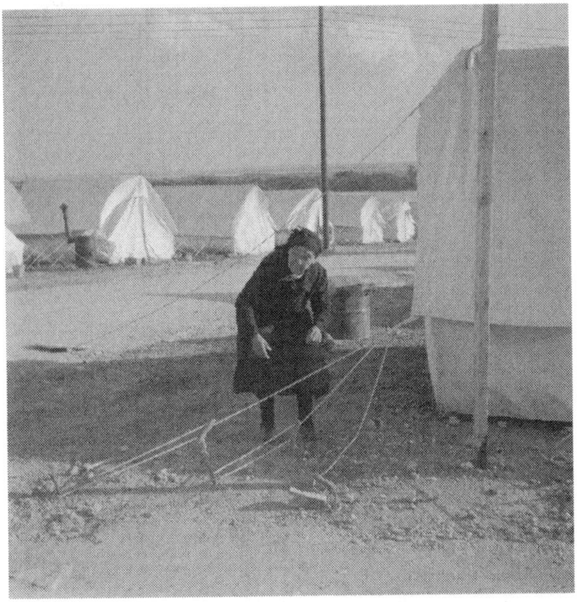

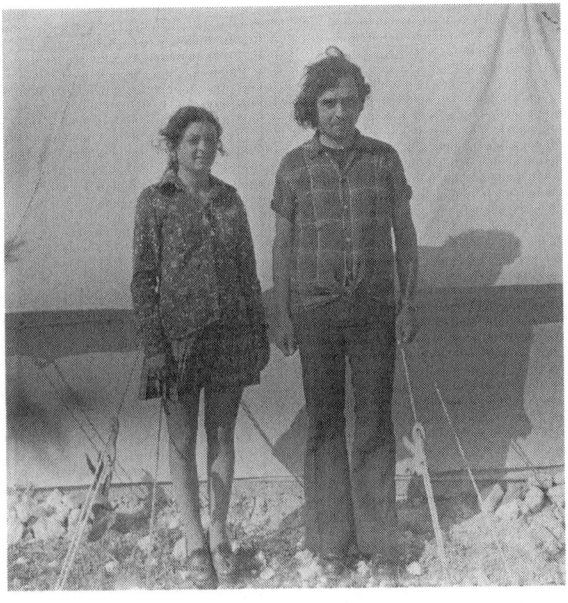

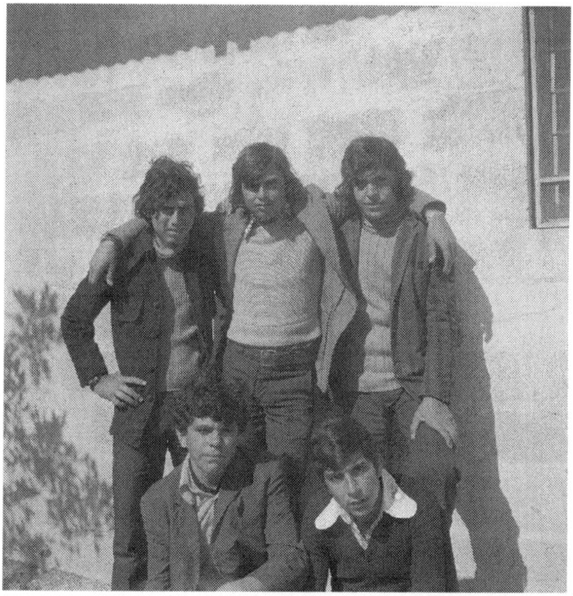

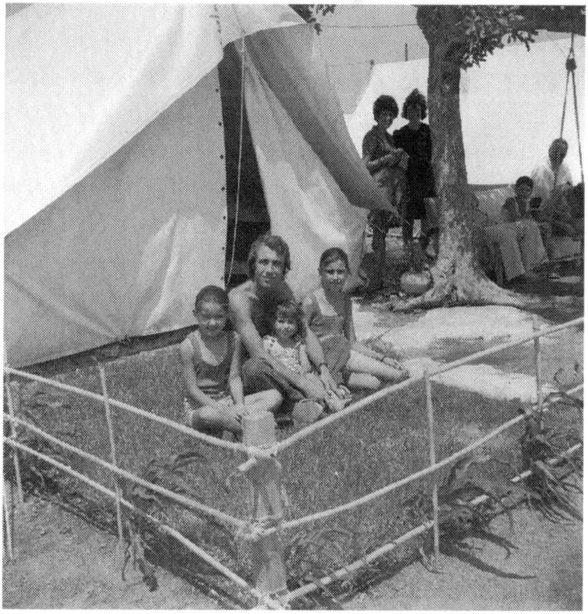

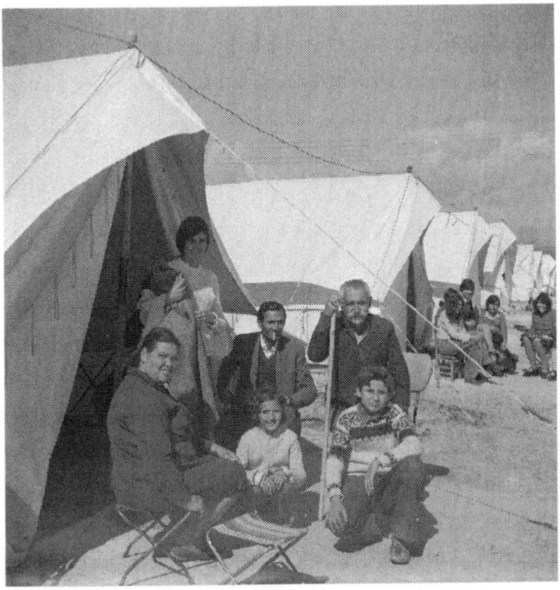

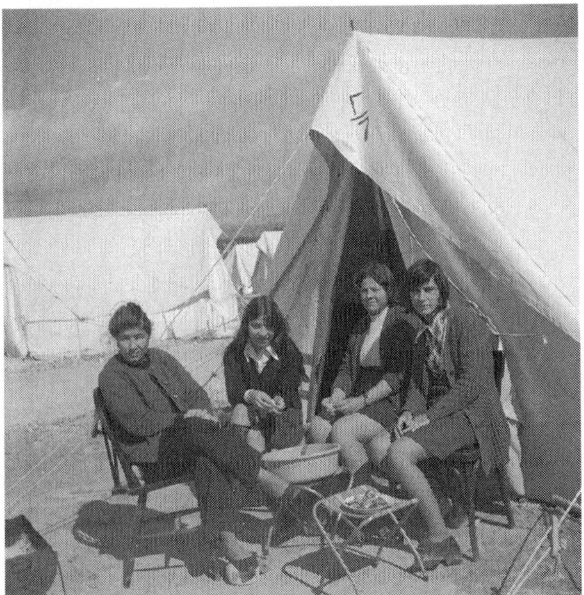

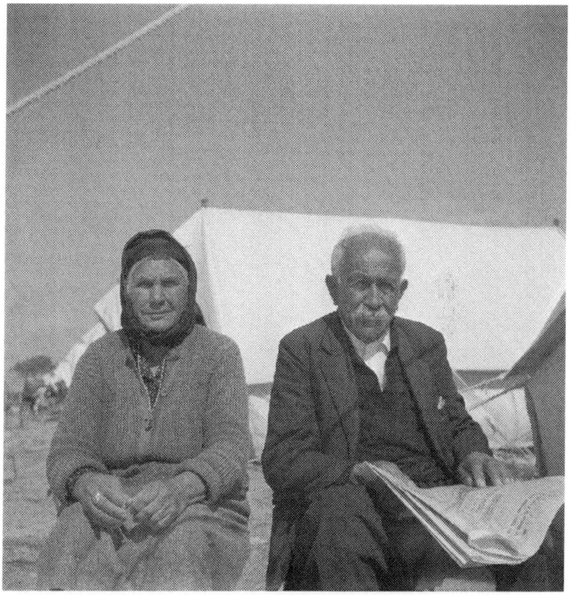

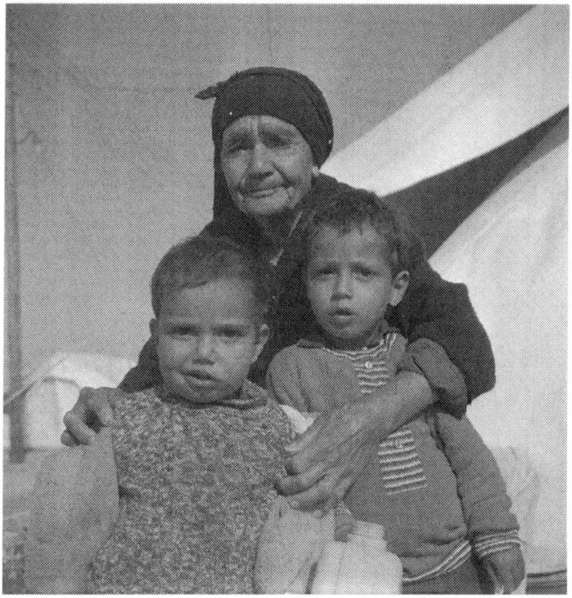

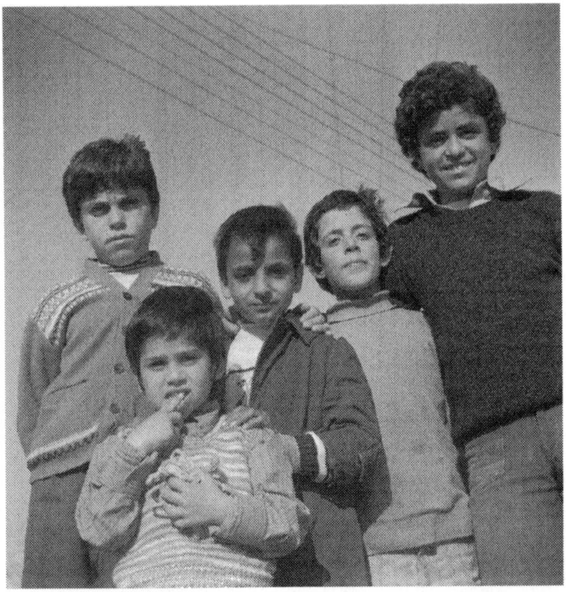

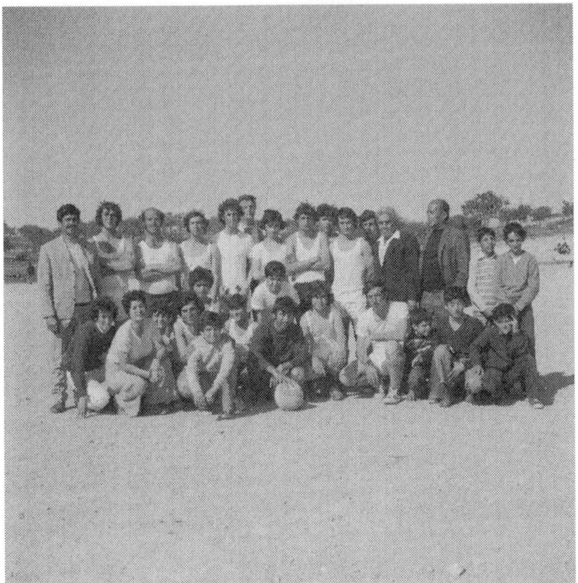

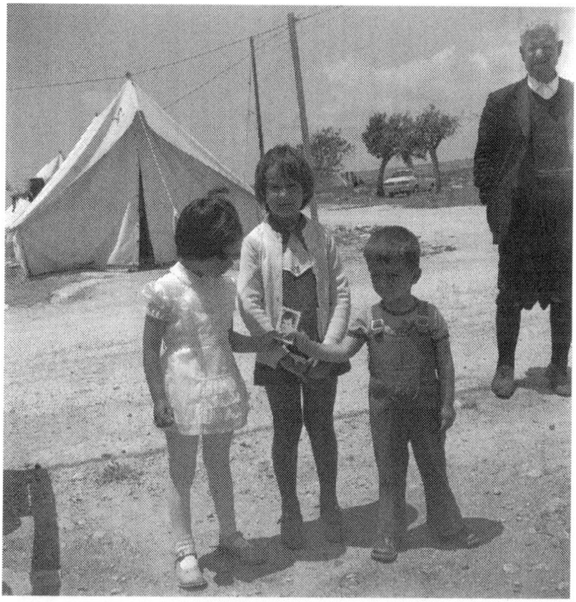

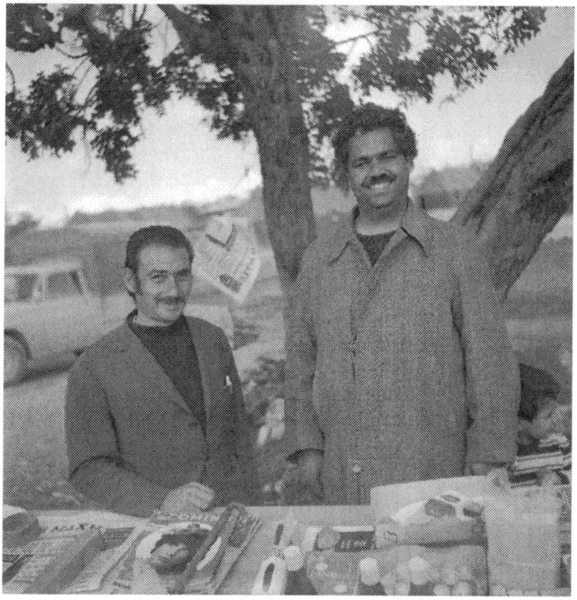

104

Coming from a different culture it was difficult for me in some situations to decide what the right course of action should be. In the story that follows I was faced with just such a dilemma.

Demos the simple man

Demos was a simple man. Unfortunately he was not simple enough to be unaware that he was the butt of jokes and easy prey to those who taunted him. I was shocked at the attitude of some of my neighbours towards those with learning difficulties and deeply upset by the events of this story but in its own terrible way what happened brought about an equilibrium in which Demos could live comfortably among his fellow refugees.

I had seen Demos and his parents arrive at the camp several months after most of us had settled there. Life in their village in the north had become unsustainable and they had been obliged to tie a few belongings into bundles and make the journey across the United Nations Green Line and into the government controlled south of the island. They arrived one evening in March just as the sun was setting and a chill hung in the sweet scented air.

Demos was dark, stocky and unshaven and wore a battered brown suit several sizes too large for him. The dark cloth hung crumpled and dull except in worn patches where it shone as dark and polished as the back of a cockroach. He sprang nimbly from the back of the red pickup truck and gazed wide-eyed about him shouting excitedly to his parents. Demos was about forty years old and suspicion deepened that no ordinary mind reasoned inside that dark head.

His parents were old and bent and dressed in the traditional black of village people. They looked like the gnarled shadows of olive trees come stiffly to life as they climbed down painfully from the back of the truck. Demos soon had the four bundles of blankets that held their possessions on the ground and the old couple sank down onto them, exhausted by the journey. They looked around in utter bewilderment at the hundreds of white tents, the concrete and corrugated iron kitchen and toilets and the whitewashed office block.

In those days most elderly villagers travelled very little. Perhaps an occasional visit to a neighbouring village for a fair or a wedding or a longer journey to a city once or twice in a lifetime. They knew their villages intimately; every tree in every field, every large rock, the best places to find mushrooms or snails or wild asparagus and all the other good things that village people value. The lives of the refugees were deeply rooted to the soil of their ancestors and it was extremely distressing for the elderly to be uprooted. It must have seemed to these two old people that they were in a foreign land and would never see their familiar home again.

After a while officials came and helped them move into tents on the eastern edge of the camp and little by little they seemed to adapt to their new life. Demos, though, did not settle in easily. There were children and adults in the camp who amused themselves by teasing or playing jokes on the few simpletons who lived there. Most of them were blissfully unaware of their situation but Demos usually understood when he was being made a fool of and responded angrily. His reactions were an added incentive to his tormentors as he provided them with greater entertainment.

Out taking photographs of family groups one Sunday morning I heard angry shouts and laughter floating across the camp from the direction of the makeshift kafenion on the far side of the road. A group of men, lounging in their chairs in the warm morning sun, were having a joke at Demos' expense. His shouts and their laughter grew louder and wilder until there was a loud roar of derision and I saw a furious Demos come running across the road towards us. Sweating in his brown suit he rushed across the field and onto the path where I stood, camera in hand, waiting for a small group of young men to arrange themselves to their satisfaction. They stopped their posing and grinned as Demos ran past them and into a nearby tent but the grins quickly evaporated when he re-emerged wild eyed with a large knife in his hand.

Warning yells went up to those in the kafenion as Demos, tormented until his self-control had snapped, ran towards them brandishing the knife. Grabbing anything to hand with which to defend themselves they kept him at bay with chairs and brooms. Fear and anger now sounded in their voices as they shouted warnings and advice to each other and to their attacker. They weren't laughing now. Eventually Demos was overpowered and dragged, still half crazy and kicking, back to his tent. Some of the men guarded him there whilst a suitable means of punishment was sought.

A burly man arrived with a length of electrical cable and Demos was subjected to a terrible beating that kept him confined to his tent for many days. There he was sympathetically nursed by his more enlightened neighbours and eventually emerged physically fully recovered. A wary eye was kept on him for a while but he became accepted into the society of the camp and I never saw him teased again.

To this day I blame myself for not trying to prevent what happened. The camp authorities felt it best to let the refugees handle such situations in their own way and I am ashamed to say that I acquiesced. It may be true that in other societies a man of Demos' instability who attacked others with a knife would have been confined to an institution for years and that his punishment on the camp was more humane but the savagery of what happened there still disturbs me greatly.

Candle setback

My plan to employ refugees making candles on the camp never got off the ground. We did make some in our small workshop (we had been forbidden to use our marquee by a visiting fire safety officer) for use in our improvised church. The refugees would burn candles as an offering for a dead loved one or to supplicate whichever saint they felt was best able to help them with the return of someone lost or missing. It seemed that the success of the candle was related to its size and we once produced a huge candle weighing several kilos for a particularly desperate mother whose son was missing.

I showed the workshop supervisor all the techniques involved in making the special citrus fruit candles and we produced many examples which were sold to the public but problems occurred finding materials and no refugees were ever employed.

Frustrated by lack of progress with candles I proposed another scheme based on a project I had used with my younger pupils in Famagusta. I planned to make small replica icons[21] using postcards stuck onto wood. This proved to be more successful and led eventually to the refugee authorities insisting I join the payroll. I received £10 a week.

---

[21] Icons: Pictures of holy individuals, especially saints, that decorate Greek and Russian Orthodox Christian Churches

ICONS

Kyrios Megalos

The icons seemed an ideal project as they were quintessentially Cypriot, relatively simple to make and all the materials were available locally. Once again I set about making a few samples and a meeting was arranged with Kyrios Photis Stavri, the Chief Accountant and Head of Stores for ΥΜΑΠΕ for the District of Limassol. This official, who in nervous anticipation of our meeting I named Kyrios Megalos (Mr Big), controlled all supplies coming from abroad and those purchased by the government and the distribution of those supplies to the refugees for the greater part of the southeast of the island. He was also responsible for the payroll of the workers and payments to suppliers. It was with some trepidation that I stood in line to be granted an interview. His office and storerooms were located in the large, newly constructed Tsirion stadium which sat in fields to the north of Limassol. The labyrinth of rooms beneath the stands were full of dried and canned foodstuffs of all kinds, clothing, bedding and simple folding beds, chairs and tables (and even coffins) and were a hive of activity. Lorries were being loaded and unloaded at a great pace and shouted instructions and banter filled the air. Surrounded by this lively mêlée I shuffled slowly forward in the crowd that formed a rough queue to the door of the great man which was guarded by one of his workers. It was hardly an orderly queue but the guard saw fair play and I was eventually ushered from the clamour and confusion outside to the quiet within.

'It's the Englishman Mr Stavri.' said the guard and as he returned to the waiting crowd closing the door behind him the clamour grew muffled.

'Please, have a seat' said Mr Megalos in perfect English gesturing to a comfortable chair in front of his desk. 'I have to make a note of something and then I will be with you.'

As I sat before him it was hard to believe that this man had been dealing with desperate individuals for hours and still had dozens outside waiting to be seen. He was intently focussed on his notes for a minute or so and then he turned his attention to me. He was surprisingly young and, leaning forward on his desk, he looked directly at me through large horn-rimmed glasses.

'I am surprised to see you, an Englishman, here in this office.' he said quietly. 'But I hear that you are trying to help us. To help the refugees.'

I explained briefly the circumstances that brought me there and went on to outline my initial scheme to make five hundred icons. Leaning back in his chair he listened attentively, his hands resting together on the desk and his head tipped back slightly, his eyes on the ceiling. Given the hubbub outside I could hardly believe I had this level of undivided attention but when I had finished he sat thinking for what seemed like an age before suddenly leaning forward.

'Right, we'll do it.' he said. 'Come back tomorrow at 10 o' clock and I'll give you a van and a driver and enough money to buy the materials.'

It was hard to believe my ears but over the following months I learned that Kyrios Megalos was a man of action, used to making quick decisions and prepared to take risks if he thought the outcome warranted it. He was the exact opposite of the stereotypical bureaucrat.

The first project

The next morning we bought wood, glue, rasps, cramps, sandpaper and postcards of various icons and these were delivered to the camp. Kyrios Stelios, the camp manager, gave his unwavering support and recruited a group of six women as our workforce. I was disappointed not to employ men but the men would only work for pay and at this stage that was unaffordable.

Using a large table from the dining marquees and a few benches we set up a simple workshop in one of spare marquees and the group assembled one morning for my demonstration of the techniques involved. In the early days of making the replica icons I used to crunch up the postcard before flattening it out again and gluing it to the wood base. This created a crackled finish when dark polish was applied later. At the time I did not realise the reverence with which devout orthodox Christians regard icons. It is as if the depiction of the saint was the saint himself and many icons have miracles attributed to them and are worshipped.

In my ignorance I started my demonstration by taking a postcard depicting John the Baptist and crunching it up into a ball in my hands. A little gasp and a low muttering rose from the assembled women and Kyrios Stelios, who had introduced me, shifted uneasily from one foot to the other. Oblivious to the upset I was causing I thoroughly disfigured the postcard scrubbing it in my hands and, to emphasise the need to break up the surface, put it on the floor and stamped on it. By now the muttering had become an excited babble and it dawned on me that something was wrong.

Kyrios Stelios's eyes were wide with alarm and he met my glance with a rapid shaking of the head. I quickly moved on to the rest of the processes and the women quietened down. Soon they were working themselves, respectfully folding the cards or carefully squeezing them in their hands and Kyrios Stelios took me to one side and pointed out my faux pas. I later abandoned the scrunching technique as it was never done thoroughly enough to be effective but the ladies proved excellent at all the other tasks and before long we had five hundred quite beautiful little icons ready to sell.

Sales

The plan was to get enough money from the sales from the pilot scheme to pay our setting up costs and finance the purchase of more wood and postcards for the next scheme and pay the refugees a small wage for their labour. We found that one hundred icons fitted perfectly into the boxes that were used to ship cans of condensed milk to the island and, with five boxes in the back of his car, I set off with Kyrios Megalos's chief accountant to try to sell them. We first called upon the companies that were contracted by the refugee services to supply essential foodstuffs: pasta, dried beans, canned milk etc. We intended to ask them to send the icons they bought to their overseas suppliers to show the world that the refugees were not idly waiting for hand-outs but were trying to help themselves. I could not fully understand the conversations we had in the offices of these companies but I could sometimes detect a certain reticence at first on the part of our would be customers which seemed to evaporate quickly and I asked my companion what he was saying that clinched the deal so often.

'I simply let them know that I'm the chief accountant', he said, 'They know that I can pay their invoices promptly or keep them on my desk for weeks.'

The scheme takes off

We sold the first batch quickly and started another, this time to make two thousand icons and to pay the workers. The original women or their men folk and other new recruits joined the team and the second batch was soon completed and sold. Another batch of three thousand and then another of ten thousand were made and I was pleased with the progress of the project because we were able to employ more and more refugees but we had begun to reach saturation point with sales. In order to boost sales a small kiosk was built on the main road where we sold not only the icons but a few candles as well. It soon became obvious though that if we were to continue with the project we would have to look at selling beyond the confines of the island.

News of the project had spread and during this period we had many visitors taking an interest in the work. Following the visit of an American diplomat and a contact with a representative of A.H.E.P.A.[22] who both offered help I had the notion that we could export icons to the U.S.A. where a huge Greek population would surely support their Cypriot brothers and sisters. It seemed feasible that, with the help of the Greek Orthodox Bishop of North America who had often pledged his support of the refugees, we could distribute icons to the churches where appeals could be made and they could be sold. I had a figure of one million in mind which would have kept the Kolossi camp and possibly others, fully employed for some time.

By now we had made fifteen and a half thousand icons and control of the project was taken from Kyrios Megalos to a newly formed committee[23] based in Nicosia. Lines of communication became stretched, decisions took longer and the project seemed to be in danger of grinding to a halt. Whilst anxious to employ refugees, it was a priority of the committee to develop the traditional handicrafts of Cyprus and the icons did not match that criterion. I fully supported the development of traditional crafts in the fullness of time but felt that in the current circumstances giving work to the refugees was more important. I managed to get permission for a batch of twenty thousand icons but was told it would be the last as sales were proving difficult. I asked to have control of sales as well as production but that was not possible and I resigned myself to the fact that I had done as much as I could and decided to leave the employ of the refugee services once I had set up the final project.

---

[22] **A.H.E.P.A.:** American Hellenic Educational Progressive Association

[23] The committee that managed the refugee handicrafts projects eventually became the Cyprus Handicraft Service which continues to flourish and does excellent work to preserve and promote traditional Cypriot handicrafts. I am proud of the small part I played in its foundation. Through their shops all the icons were eventually sold either directly to the public or to tourist outlets

The final project

We had six different icons and employed six groups of five to seven people; each group being responsible for a particular icon. I was delighted when, on hearing of my resignation as project manager, a group that I knew well asked me to join them and I happily accepted. By now everyone knew the techniques well and each group operated like a well-oiled machine. Groups were paid for each finished icon so the desire to complete was strong and I had set up rigorous checks to make sure that quality did not suffer. My erstwhile colleagues took over the running of the project and did the checking and burnt on the branding which every icon eventually had on its back. Today there are many replica icons on the market but most of the genuine Kolossi Camp products are stamped with a brand that reads along these lines: "This icon was made by refugees in Kolossi Refugee Camp using timber from the forests of Cyprus burned in the Turkish invasion of 1974"

The processes were simple: glue was applied to the pre-cut wood base and the card stuck on; about twenty-five icons were placed in a stack into a cramp and tightly compressed until the glue dried; the edges were then rasped and sandpapered to obliterate the square edges and the distinction between card and wood; dark wax polish was then applied and the front edges were blackened over a smoky candle: finally the whole icon was given a good polish with a scrap of cloth.

We worked in one of the large khaki marquees and it was very hot. By now it was high summer and we sweltered in the smoky atmosphere, the stuffiness made worse by having to keep all the flaps closed so that the candle flames burned steadily. To keep up spirits our conversations usually drifted to discussing how the money we earned would be spent and to planning trips to the beach for picnics. Thoughts of immersing oneself gently into a cool sea and of eating delicious meat and fish cooked over charcoal on a beach in the quiet of the evening were so potent and comforting they kept us going through countless hours of sweated labour.

Demetrios's dilemma

We laughed often and stories would pass from group to group around the marquee. Typical of the rough, sometimes cruel, humour was the plight of poor Demitrios, a short young man who was hopelessly in love with Yiannoula, the tall willowy daughter of one of our workers. We heard that he had tentatively approached the father to see if his advances would be welcome. He was told that a race could be arranged where the girl would be given a start of ten metres and that if Demitrios could catch her within five minutes he would have the father's blessing. Poor Demitrios could visualise the scenario that was the cause of so much mirth: his short legs pumping furiously while the girl swiftly widened the gap between them. He never took up the challenge.

Costas Kelis's shirt

An incident that had the whole marquee roaring with laughter was that of Costas Kelis's shirt. Costas had the nickname 'Kelis' because he was bald, 'Keleh' being the slang for head. He was in his late twenties and was known for being very particular about his appearance, always dressing as smartly as possible and spending any spare money he had on clothes. He would even arrive to work on the icons immaculately dressed. One afternoon the stifling air of the marquee was rent by his strangulated scream.

'Bougamiso mou!' ('My shirt!').

Costas was looking in horror at the scrap of cloth in his hand with which he had been polishing an icon. He had gradually recognised its pattern as that of the new shirt that he had worn that morning but had taken off in an attempt to keep cool. Any donated clothing that came to the camp that was faulty was given to us to be torn into rags. Unfortunately Costas had placed his shirt too close to the bag containing these clothes. In the dim light someone had mistaken it for an old shirt and his once proud garment was now a collection of small pieces of cloth scattered over the workbenches. He wandered from bench to bench picking up the fragments, lamenting his loss and wearing an expression of bewildered sorrow. As we all gradually realised what had happened the laughter grew louder and louder until even Costas Kelis himself, standing in the middle of the workshop with scraps of his precious shirt in both hands, broke into a broad smile and joined in the uproar.

Yiorgos 'Belos'

Eventually the project was completed, the last icon made, inspected and stamped and packed into its box. We congratulated ourselves on a job well done and waited to be paid. Unfortunately the wheels of the system ground rather slowly and after several days the teams became impatient for their money. Yiorgos 'Belos' (Crazy George) decided to take the matter into his own hands and stormed into the workshop and grabbed a box of icons. Threatening to take them to Limassol and sell them in the streets he roared off in his dilapidated car in a cloud of dust. There were grim mutterings about the seriousness of stealing government property and the consequences for Yiorgos but it transpired that he had only taken his booty to a remote part of the camp and it was soon recovered. It may have been a coincidence but soon after that we were all paid.

Yiorgos 'Belos' was a very likeable, chaotic young man. It was rumoured that he had won the state lottery before the war and the money had gone to his head. He had been in prison at the time of the invasion but had been released along with other minor offenders to help fight the Turks. In prison he was taught pyrographic techniques with which to create decorative gourds using traditional designs and, out of the blue one day, he proudly gave me one of these as a gift. I was sad to hear a few years later that he had been killed whilst working on a ship that struck a mine when passing through the Suez Canal, but Yiorgos was not the kind of man to die quietly in his bed.

Roadblock at Ypsonas

I had a brush with the police myself returning to the camp from Limassol late one night when I was stopped at a roadblock in the village of Ypsonas. At that time the Cyprus government was trying to prevent the smuggling of Turkish Cypriots to the north of the island and vehicles were randomly stopped and searched as a matter of course.

The police officers manning the barrier became suspicious when they opened the boot of my battered VW Beetle and found several boxes filled with icons. There were many reports in the media at that time about an illegal trade in Orthodox icons taken from churches in the Turkish held area and sold to buyers in Western Europe and the USA.

'What is this?' one of the young policemen muttered, pulling an icon from its wooden box.

'It's not a real icon.' I said struggling to find the right words in Greek. 'It's not authentic.'

He wasn't convinced and called another officer from the office.

'These are icons, look Pavlos, hundreds of them.'

'From where did you take these icons?' said the third officer with a touch of anger in his voice. It was clear that, notwithstanding the fact that my icons were so small and that there were multiple icons of identical designs, I was suspected of being part of the smuggling trade.

'We make these in Kolossi refugee camp.' I said, becoming a little alarmed. At first I had found the situation amusing but now their growing animosity had me worried.

'You are an Englishman. Yes? And you say you stay in the refugee camp? Show me your identification.' He clearly didn't believe me and the fact that I had forgotten to carry my refugee card did not help matters.

'Look at these icons.' I pleaded. 'There are lots all the same, they cannot be authentic.'

He fixed me with a hard, disbelieving stare.

'Tell me again how you say you come to have these in your car.'

I repeated my story but they found the explanation that I was an English refugee living in Kolossi camp helping other refugees make replica icons totally implausible. Although anxious I was quietly pleased that our icons were so well made that they looked authentic enough to fool these officers.

It looked like being a long night but then I remembered that the camp had recently been allocated a policeman to sleep there overnight. He had been given a tiny room next to the office and a hole had been knocked through the adjoining wall just big enough for him to reach through to the telephone. Luckily I had the camp number with me.

The officers were on the point of ringing their superiors to decide what to do with me but I persuaded them to first ring the camp. It took a painfully long time for the policeman at the camp to answer and he was clearly a little sleepy as the Ypsonas officer had to repeat my unlikely story twice. I breathed a sigh of relief as the expression on his face changed gradually from scepticism to incredulity to happy satisfaction. The attitude of the officers changed completely and I was suddenly transformed from villain to hero. They re-examined the icons and congratulated me on how well they had been made, asking me to explain the techniques used. Basking in my new-found status I was pleased to do so and after a few minutes of showing off was sent on my way with cheerful waves and good wishes for the success of our project.

Branding the finished icons

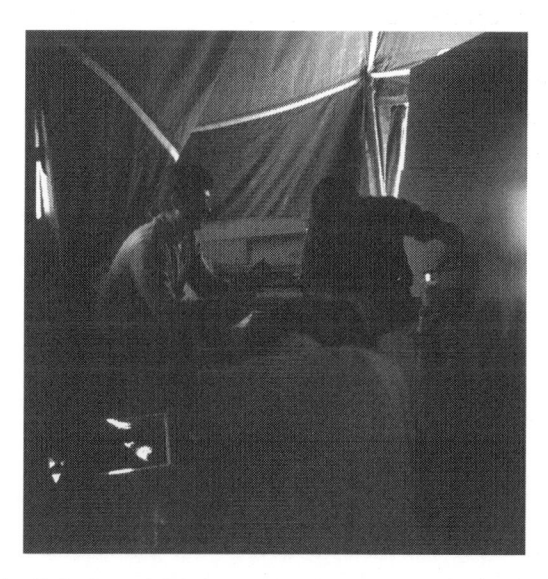

With all the flaps closed the marquee became very hot and stuffy

The workshop showing smoking, polishing and quality control

Team members pose with their icons

Chapter 6 - LEAVING THE CAMP

The government of Cyprus had resisted the idea that the island should be divided into two zones with Turkish Cypriots in the north and Greek Cypriots in the south and had taken whatever measures they could to prevent what is now called 'ethnic cleansing'. By late 1975 however, with winter coming on and with little prospect of a return to their homes, it was reluctantly decided to move the refugees into the villages deserted by the Turks.

The houses in these villages had fallen into disrepair and most had been stripped of anything useful. Divested of doors, windows and roof tiles the houses needed major renovation before they were ready to be occupied. In this process each house was given a number which was daubed on the wall next to the door in green paint.

Many people in our camp were allocated houses in the nearby village of Kantou and it was with mixed feelings of anticipation and resignation that they set off on a bus one morning to discover how lucky they had been in the allocation lottery. Stepping down from the bus in this unfamiliar village, clutching a paper indicating their number, each family now went in search of their allocated house.

To many this was a tragic moment. They now had to face the reality that they would not soon, and maybe never, return to their homes. In a sense a swap had been done; the Turks now lived in their homes and they were now to live in the homes of the Turks.

Some fared better than others and I admired the good natured, stoic manner with which those less fortunate accepted their lot. There was even friendly banter among the men over who had the better property and comforting hands were placed on the shoulders of those who were disappointed.

Little by little the camp emptied and we decided that it was time for us to go too. Although our friends wanted us to move with them to Kantou, we felt that we should not occupy a house that a more needy refugee might want and so rented a house near the centre of Limassol. Surprised by how many things we had accumulated we packed them into our VW Beetle and closed our tents for the last time.

It was an emotional moment. This place had become our home. We had known good days and bad days, tears and laughter. We had seen the seasons change from the cold and wet of winter to the sledgehammer heat of summer and now autumn was putting a chill into the air again in the evenings. Zim always enjoyed riding on the running boards of the beetle on the dirt tracks of the camp. His favourite trick was to jump off while the car was still moving and roll on the ground in imitation of characters in a film he had seen. He took a last ride now as we made our way slowly through the half empty camp shouting goodbye to the few friends who were still there.

The rains came and the once dusty roads between the abandoned tents were soon high in weeds. Only a few diehards who refused to move remained and unattended guy ropes slackened, canvas flaps slapped loosely in the wind and the camp kitchen and office, once the hubs of camp life, stood empty and abandoned. Goats grazed outside the old kafenion kiosk where I had once sat and listened to endless debate and speculation.

In the months that followed I often stopped on my way past the camp and wandered among the abandoned tents remembering the days that we had seen there. I passed the tent where the boy who used to borrow my bicycle to go to work in Limassol had lived; the marquee where we sweated together to

Unattended guy ropes slackened and canvas flaps slapped loosely in the wind

make over thirty three thousand icons; the tent where Demos had lain for a week recovering from his beating. A posse of little ghosts with Zim among them ran in front of me to the washrooms intent upon some mischief or other swiftly overtaking the bent old lady with a bad back whose name I could never remember.

I told myself that the refugees were better off now than they had been when there but part of me was sad. The inevitable move into Turkish properties marked a further slide into the permanent division of the island and I had a premonition that that division would last for many years.

In the fullness of time permanent bungalows were built to replace the tents and sadly they are still occupied by refugees today. The western edge of the camp where our family once lived has become a smart neighbourhood of stylish villas and I would like to think that some of them may be occupied by refugees from the camp. I hope that those that live there, whoever they may be, are as content as I was back in 1975 when, despite the hardship and sadness, the indomitable spirit of the people never failed to gladden my heart. For that the refugees of Cyprus have my everlasting gratitude.

Photo: Ramin Habibi

Tom, May, myself and Zim 2012

POSTSCRIPT

In the autumn of 1975 I returned to full-time art teaching, initially sharing my week between the Foley's Grammar School in Limassol and St. John's School in Episkopi.

We settled into life in Limassol and discovered we were only a few streets away from Photis Stavri (Kyrios Megalos) and his family and we became good friends. Before long our good friends Photis and Yana Photiou from Famagusta returned to the island and Photis re-established his architects practice. In the fullness of time Eas and Jason qualified as architects and the three of them now run a very successful business in Limassol.

By 1977 I was teaching full-time at the Foley's School and had a number of pen and ink drawings on the market which sold very well. In April of that year our second son, Thomas, was born.

In 1980 we moved to the abandoned Turkish village of Plataniskia[24] and the life we enjoyed there would fill another book. Being rather remote very few refugees wanted to move there and we did not feel we were depriving anyone needier. Our arrival swelled the population of the village to twenty eight.

I was able to acquire a small studio and construct a wood burning kiln in the hill beside our house to develop my ceramic work. Successful exhibitions followed and I gave up part of my teaching to devote more time to my own work.

In 1988 we decided to move to England for a year to enable me to study full-time at Goldsmiths' College in London for a postgraduate diploma in ceramics. After successfully completing the course we were planning to return to Cyprus but the death of my father resulted in a change of plan and we decided to stay in England for a while. That while stretched to twenty two years and we had to give up our home in Plataniskia. I became a senior lecturer at a college in Suffolk and eventually gained an MA for practising artists from the University of East Anglia.

On retirement in 2009 May and I went travelling, spending almost a year in the southern hemisphere visiting Australia and New Zealand and Thailand where Tom had followed in Zim's footsteps and was working as an English teacher.

In 2010 we decided to go looking for a place to settle abroad and drove for months through France, Spain, Portugal and Italy seeing many beautiful places but without seeing anywhere we really loved. We decided to take a boat to Cyprus to see old friends and I soon realised that I had been trying to find a replacement for 'the old country' in all our travels.

Cyprus is a very different country now to the one we left in 1988 and even more different than that in which we first

---

[24] Plataniskia is now a thriving village and houses a fine Printmaking Museum established by the renowned artist, Hambis, himself now a resident of the village.

arrived in 1972. There is a magic that remains, however, that I find impossible to define. It's a combination of the land, the flora and fauna, the history and the people. We now live in a small village in the hills in the west of the island where our Cypriot neighbours are amazed that we speak a little Greek and the local shop owner always insists we sit down for a-coffee whenever we visit.

Thanks to the magic of Google Earth we can clearly see the home we left in Famagusta in 1974. The city has remained unoccupied now for almost forty years and the buildings have suffered badly. Sadly the red tiled roof of our house has almost completely gone and the internal structure of the building is clearly visible. It is a bitter-sweet experience to identify the rooms and reminisce about what we did within those now exposed walls.

England is my mother country and I love her like a mother; she has always been there and it is all too easy to take her for granted. My love for Cyprus is more like the love for a wife; you remember a time without her and once you've found her and fallen in love with her she's in your blood forever.

Printed in Great Britain
by Amazon.co.uk, Ltd.,
Marston Gate.